Lambourn

LAMBOURN
Village of Racing

Alan Lee

Arthur Barker Limited   London
A subsidiary of Weidenfeld (Publishers) Limited

*To my wife Trish
and to the good people of Lambourn.
They all had to put up with me
in the making of this book.*

Published in Great Britain by
Arthur Barker Limited
91 Clapham High Street
London SW4 7TA

ISBN 0 213 16852 9

Typeset by Deltatype, Ellesmere Port
Printed in Great Britiain by
Butler & Tanner Ltd
Frome and London

Contents

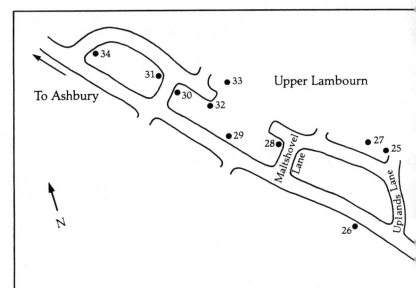

To Ashbury

Upper Lambourn

Maltshovel Lane

Uplands Lane

Folly Road

1 The George	18 Church
2 The Red Lion	19 Chemist — wine store
3 Parish Council	20 Freddie Maxwell
4 Ladbroke's	21 British Legion
5 Newsagent's	22 Odds 'n' Jods
6 Garage	23 The Lamb
7 Saddlers	24 Jim Cramsie
8 L.R.T. Horseboxes	25 Fred Winter
9 Sports Club	26 Reg Akehurst
10 Barry Hills	27 Fulke Walwyn
11 John Francome	28 The Maltshovel
12 Nick Henderson	29 Martin O'Halloran
13 Vet	30 Nick Vigors
14 John Rodbourn	31 Nick Gaselee
15 Blacksmith	32 Cruck Cottage
16 Stan Mellor	33 Richard Head
17 Peter Walwyn	34 Jenny Pitman

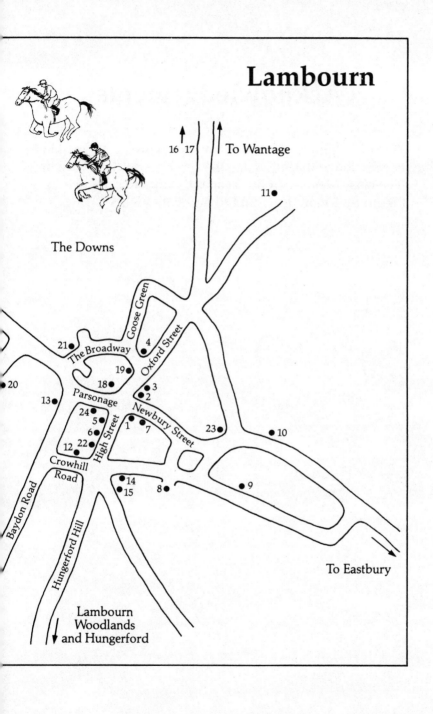

Lambourn

16 17 | To Wantage

11●

The Downs

Goose Green

21●
The Broadway

4●
Oxford Street

20●

19●

18●
Parsonage

13●

3●
2●

24●
5●
6●
22●
12●
High Street

Newbury Street

1●
7●

23●

10●

Crowhill Road

14●
15●
8●

9●

Baydon Road

Hungerford Hill

To Eastbury

Lambourn
Woodlands
and Hungerford

Acknowledgements

The photographs in this book are reproduced by kind permission of the following: Jim Cramsie, Michael Haslam, Nicholas Meyjes, John Nugent, Cressida Pemberton-Pigott, Sport and General Ltd and Pats Vigors.

Introduction

THE horse had won and the village meant to celebrate. Most of the lads had put a few bob on it, of course, just as they would with any good tip for a local animal; the win would pay for the night's beer and smokes, maybe tomorrow's too. As for the rest of the village folk, well, they were just happy about the result because they knew the trainer, the jockey, the owner and the lad who does the horse. They knew them all as friends.

If it was worth celebrating, it was worth celebrating well. Everyone agreed on that point. And what better way to give vent to the village's excitement than to ring the church bells. It seemed the perfect solution, but there was one drawback. The vicar objected, and everybody knew it.

Never mind. It was too good a day to worry about that. The usual bell-ringers, the fellows who practised two nights a week and then did the job each Sunday morning . . . they knew the way into the church, the back way of course. It was the work of a few moments to get them all inside, stifle the giggles – for one or two had enjoyed a little ale already – and then pull, pull, pull.

It was great while it lasted, but on the way back to the Red Lion they saw him. The vicar, looking stern and angry. He rounded up the bell-ringers and soon it was their ears that were ringing. Every one of them was summoned before the magistrates next morning – breach of the peace, breaking and entering, and other such things were spoken of. Not pleasant for the lads.

The following Sunday in church, the vicar preached a sermon the like of which no one had heard before. Still angry, and unable to restrain his indignation, he preached

1

at great length about the abuses of the turf and the evils to which it led. There were a few remorseful faces. Perhaps ringing the bells for the horse's win had not been the great idea it seemed. In any case, nobody seemed keen to do it again, the next time a local horse came up.

Nothing much changes. Clandestine bell-ringing, angry vicars and anti-racing sermons may be a thing of the past, but the village is still besotted by horses, still ready to throw a party, blow a week's wages and collect a mighty hangover on the strength of a local win in Saturday's big race.

It was 130 years ago that the then vicar of Lambourn, Robert Milman, took those unfortunate miscreants to the magistrate and then bent the collective ears of his Sunday congregation in an attempt to divert them from misguided lives. That story has lived on in the village from then, the 1850s, to today. But whatever other good works the Rev. Robert Milman achieved in the parish, he appears to have been distinctly unsuccessful in his efforts to turn Lambourn against its heritage.

Lambourn is horse-racing. It is known for nothing else, and probably never will be. The industrial age, to a large extent, has passed by this little village; despite the influx of commuters in the guise of city accountants, airline pilots and company directors, the business of Lambourn continues to revolve almost exclusively around the racing game and its ancillary services.

There are dissenters, of course. Aren't there always? But the majority of modern antipathy towards racing is concocted by those who have only recently moved into the village and, to be blunt, should either have done their homework more thoroughly or found somewhere else to live. Horses have been in Lambourn for hundreds of years, growing in numbers with each passing year. Fred Winter, whose racing name has become as synonymous with Lambourn as has Morecambe's name with Wise, reflects that the horse population has trebled in the eighteen years he has used the village as his base for sending out winners. The same claim is heard elsewhere and, it must be said, not everyone relishes the increase in either horseflesh or humans. Some still hanker after the days of the ancient, secluded market town described in the 1924 edition of the *Victoria County History of Berkshire*. This book explains a probable roman occupation of Lambourn, speaks of the two famous roads running through the parish – the Ridgeway, four miles north, and Ermine Street, two miles south – and adds: 'The town is in form only a large village with its church in the centre . . .' Still the case today.

It goes on: 'The ancient parish covered 14,880 acres of high downland, broken only by the valley of the Lambourn running south-east across it. In the valley and in the centre of the parish is the town of Lambourn. Uplambourn (now Upper Lambourn) lies to the north-west, at the source of the stream, and Eastbury, the third village, is lower down the valley. Till the opening of the Lambourn Valley railway in 1898, this was a very lonely and secluded part of the county. The roads which meet at Lambourn are not important highways, and its market seems to have had no time of great prosperity. The principal industry at the present day is the training of racehorses.'

Delving deeper into history, it appears that the first available mention of Lambourn occurred in King Alfred's will. He left the village, plus the neighbouring market town of Wantage, to his wife, but it subsequently reverted to the Crown. Even to someone like me, whose yen for history is so deep that I needed heavy and reluctant cramming to scrape a GCE pass, the origin of placenames is interesting, and Lambourn appears to have a number of possibilities. It has been spelt in a variety of ways through the years – Lamburne, Lambourne, Lamborne, and finally Lambourn – but the favourite explanation is that it was first spelt Lambes-bourn referring to the sheep and the burn, or stream, running through the valley.

For some years, Lambourn was not only a centre of training establishments but of racing itself. As far back as March 1779, the *London Evening Post*, long since deceased, referred to a meeting held at Lambourn the previous week. The races, each apparently over four miles, were staged at Weathercock Down, to the north-west of the village, and the Red Lion Hotel, still very much alive, was used as a headquarters for accepting entries. Whether these meetings were a frequent occurrence or not, no racing has taken place on the downs around Lambourn for over a hundred years. A pity, really, because in these days of recession and falling attendances, it is surely one of the few places were guaranteed interest could be commanded.

Every one of the trainers in the area, and they now approach forty in number, must owe a debt of gratitude to the Nugent family – landowners, businessmen and, in the case of Sir Hugh Nugent, long since retired to Ireland, a significant force in the spread of racing through the area. Sir Hugh, whose sons David and John remain among the best-known figures in Lambourn today, initiated the biggest and most-used gallops on the Downs. In the 1920s and 1930s he was also responsible for encouraging farmers and landowners to renovate derelict farmhouses – victims of the agricultural depression – and make them fit for use as training bases. Many of Lambourn's best-known trainers are even now operating from such properties.

Trainers, however, form just one of the categories of racing folk living in Lambourn. There are the jockeys, from the jumping champion John Francome and the American whizzkid flat rider Steve Cauthen, down to the many struggling for rides. There are the various ancillary essentials – the vets, saddler, blacksmiths, dentists, land-lords. And there is the fullest category of them all, the stable-lads. If often seemed to me, during the winter of

1981–2, that every other person I saw in the village was a lad, either of the traditional flat-capped and bow-legged miniature variety, or the younger, brasher but still amusingly likeable kind. Each one, I discovered, had stories worth telling; very few were disenchanted with their existence. Most, too, had routines which were regular if not quite ordered; life, to a large extent, revolved around backing winners and drinking pints, effectively combined with the unsociable but generally unnoticed twilight hours of their job.

Like all good villages, Lambourn has its communal focal points. Its church, St Michael's, looming large over the square, is still certainly among them although to a decreasing degree which many find regrettable. On the opposite side of the square stand the two largest village pubs, the Red Lion and the George, split by the Eastbury road and a generation gap, but both well-attended watering-holes. Further down the road towards Wantage lies the Memorial Hall and council office, where the rosy-cheeked clerk Gillian Jenkins listens to the complaints and problems of her flock. Then, on the corner and opposite the chemist's which doubles up as a wine store to the admitted delight of one F. Winter, is the business with guaranteed trade six days a week, fifty-two weeks a year: Ladbroke's. Their thriving custom is to be expected in such an equine stronghold, but the opposition lurking at their door is perhaps not . . . but then therein lies a tale to be told later in these pages.

Up the main street, on the road which becomes Hungerford Hill, are the principal shops of the village. The butcher's, with its welcoming window display and the sausages which are so in demand from John Francome, among others. The newsagents, where one shelf is piled with the *Sporting Life* and several others with the sweets on which stable-lads habitually gorge themselves. And the post office, which looks antiquated from the outside and confirms the impression in its musty, narrow service area.

Despite its high rate of successful productivity in terms of races won, there is never anything frenzied about life in Lambourn. Whatever the time of day or night, the pace remains constantly low-gear, perhaps because there are no major roads running through the place and, in any case, many of the stable-lads have no car. Always, there appear to be plenty of people walking the streets, plenty more standing around as if waiting for a tip.

It would be misleading, however, to give the impression that everyone in the vicinity is in love with horses. The majority, certainly. But the exceptions to any rule rarely go unnoticed, and in a recent court case heard by Lambourn magistrates, an unemployed man living in Upper Lambourn claimed that he did not turn up for appointments with his probation officer because he was frightened of the racehorses passing outside his front door. There is no disputing the fact that horses can intimidate. They are big, they have sharp teeth and hooves which can cause no end of damage and inconvenience if kicked in the right direction. Not being from racing stock myself, I confess I trod a little warily, trying hard to regulate my movements and give the impression of complete relaxation, when first I stepped inside a race-horse's box. The Lambourn experience has cured me of most such apprehensions.

Lambourn certainly possesses a quite unique spirit of togetherness. With so many of the inhabitants working towards similar ends, the conversation is predictable yet lively, narrow but witty. There is also an immense amount of loyalty; friendships are earned and then guarded.

Not that the place escapes the seamier sides of life. The hooligan element may be less rife than elsewhere, but there are occasional acts of destruction committed among the stableyards, and in February vandals even dug up the cricket square at the village sports club. Walking the streets at night is not, however a hazardous exercise in Lambourn. Listen to many of the wags of the place, indeed, and one could believe that the entire village is far too busy with other nocturnal activities to be causing trouble. It was impossible to keep count of the number of times I was advised, with the accompaniment of a nudge and a wink, to call this book *Sin City*.

The folk I met in the course of my winter at Lambourn ranked, with very few exceptions, among the friendliest and most genuine I have known. This is their story, necessarily incomplete because it would need a series of books to satisfy every character in this endless cast, but hopefully close enough to the truth about a village which is unique.

1·Hours of Agony, Moments of Glory

NICK Henderson rummaged vaguely in a cupboard and pulled out a packet of ginger nuts. Slinging them on the table with an apologetic grin, he muttered something about not being very good in the kitchen, then peered into the teapot and, satisfied with the brew, poured it into two cups.

'Making tea,' he said with a mischievous, mock disparagement, 'is the one thing Fred Winter taught me.'

Neatly dressed, precise of movement and conversation, one could easily have mistaken Henderson for a city gent . . . which is exactly what he would have been on that afternoon in October 1981 if he had followed his family's direction rather than his private instincts. Wincing slightly at what he clearly thought a fortunate escape, Henderson fidgetted and checked his watch. It was five-thirty in the evening and he was impatient to be underway with evening stables at the neat, fifty-horse yard he had built up within three years to one of the most thriving National Hunt concerns in the country. But he had time to recall the six months he had spent in the city, virtually as a matter of course after leaving school. 'My career there seemed to have been mapped out for me, but I knew it would not last long. They would not have known what to make of me there.'

Born only a few miles from Lambourn, and fascinated from childhood by the racing world unfolding around him, Henderson rode over jumps as an amateur for six years, his successes including the prestigious Foxhunter's Chase at Liverpool. Then he graduated to 'the other side', as assistant trainer to the legendary figure who in fact taught him a great deal more than how to make tea. After three years, he felt ready to go it alone and so, in July 1978, at the relatively tender age of twenty-seven Henderson was granted a trainer's licence and established himself in Windsor House, a vividly yellow building which catches the eye and the imagination as you descend Hungerford Hill into Lambourn village.

Henderson had just begun his fourth season as a trainer, and did not need reminding it was an important one. The virus, that most deadly of all evils in a trainer's black book, had struck viciously the previous year to curtail his progress, cut off his flow of winners. Mix that with the poor luck which seemed to dog those good horses which escaped, and the brew was virtually enough to choke the yard. But despair, in racing, lasts only until the next winner – or, at worst, the next season and as we left the kitchen of Windsor House and crunched out on to the gravel, Henderson was not short of confidence for the campaign which was even now beginning to shake off the laziness of the August–September warm-up and settle down to proper business.

His walk is brisk and purposeful, he has wide eyes which can transmit humour or anxiety with equal facility, and he has a nervous habit of running his fingers back through his fine fair hair. In short, Nick is a worrier.

'I think we all are in this business,' he says, 'but there are degrees. I do worry a lot. There is really no escape from the job. I am up at 6.30 every morning and from then to the time I go to bed again, I am thinking about the horses. During the evenings, when people in other jobs can usually relax, my time and attentions are always taken up by phone calls. Owners come on the phone at all hours. I can understand their interest, and it would certainly do me no good to discourage it, but I do sometimes wish they would give it a rest at nights. My wife Di tells me to take the thing off the hook, but I daren't. It just might be something important I'm missing.'

With widespread hope and pride, and occasional scepticism, Henderson introduced me to each of his charges, commenting on their breeding, past form and prospects. He knew each horse as if they were children in a school class, and like all teachers, he had his favourite pets and those he considered a little errant.

Our companion on the tour of each box was Nick's head lad, 'Corky' Browne, a small, weatherbeaten archetypal racing man who carried a saucepan full of carrots with which Henderson fed each horse in turn. 'Corky' managed to remain deadpan, while injecting humour into each situation. He jocularly offered me the ride on Bowshot, a notoriously adventurous jumper, at Wincanton the following day. I did not like to confess that my credentials – one uncomfortable hour bouncing on the back of a mountain pony on the Kashmir slopes of the Himalayas – were not impressive. We circled the new block of stables, built just two years ago as the Henderson operation expanded, then returned to the house via the equine swimming pool which lies as the *pièce de résistance* of the yard. Beneficial to horses with any leg ailments, major or minor, it is much in demand by surrounding trainers, but Henderson rarely charges hard cash. 'In this village,' he explains, 'favours are exchanged readily. There are always things we can do for each other, and if we were not on decent terms, it could become an intolerable place.'

That, it clearly is not. Henderson is part of a social set which involves various other trainers, both on the flat and National Hunt, and jockeys such as the current champion, John Francome. It is a convivial circle which meets regularly for food, conversation and the odd drink, though as Henderson smilingly explained, it hardly qualifies for the jibes of 'gin and tonic set' hurled at it by one or two less sociable members of the village community. 'People may think we are boring, us trainers. It is true that we see each other every day in the course of working, and that a lot of us meet often to have drinks and dinner together. But we have a lot in common, and we might as well enjoy our lifestyle. Otherwise, we shall all go quickly mad.'

We returned to the house, dallied in the outer office, where Nick's secretary Sandra was dealing with the entries' book, then wandered through into the comfortable sitting-room. A small dog, something of a trademark among racing trainers I had found, settled itself on my lap as soon as I sank into an easy chair with one of those gins and tonic, but Nick was not ready to relax.

He sat on the upright chair at his desk, where the telephone console light glared at him balefully. He glared back briefly, as if daring it to ring. It did, and the query was answered efficiently. He got up, fiddled with the TV controls, then sat down again and toyed with the edges of a large notebook, chatting amicably but with his deepest thoughts clearly elsewhere.

On the table in front of me lay the tell-tale signs of a mind which needed relaxing – a rubicube and crib and noughts-and-crosses boards. Up at the desk, Nick had turned to talking jockeys, and the inevitable Francome, his contemporary and friend. 'He is out on his own, a genius in the saddle,' he said. 'And I told Fred so the other morning,' he added, lapsing once more into mischievous pokes at his much-respected former employer.

The door of the French windows opened and bags full of packages preceded Diana Henderson, daughter of the sport's greatest Corinthian, John Thorne, and Nick's wife since 1978. Di deposited the shopping, mainly presents for the wealth of forthcoming racing weddings in the vicinity, accepted a drink and lowered herself gently into a chair. She was seven months pregnant with their first child.

I left as darkness was beginning to fall over Lambourn.

Nick walked to the gates with me, peering into one or two boxes on the way. 'I try not to wander about among the horses late at night,' he said. 'But sometimes, if I have things on my mind, it is hard to resist.'

Half a mile from Windsor House, I sat in an elegant, luxurious lounge waiting for Nick Henderson's best friend. He strode in presently, sweater and boots topped off by a cigar. He made directly for the telephone, barking a few instructions into the mouthpiece, then swore violently before allowing himself a slow smile. Barry Hills was having another trying morning.

It did not matter a fig that the flat season was just ending, and his string of 112 horses were now off the course until the end of March. A trainer's work is never done, and the present crisis – a minor molehill, really, over alterations in vaccination regulations – was just one of many to be tackled on the day I had chosen to call.

Barrington William Hills is one of two principal characters, Peter Walwyn being the other, who bely the generally held impression that Lambourn is as dominated by National Hunt centres as is Newmarket by flat-racing yards. Hills and Walwyn, in fact, each have more horses than any of the village's jumping stables, and it is their presence which ensures life and competitive interest at Lambourn the year round.

Hills lives at South Bank, which lies on the narrow, winding road out of the village towards Eastbury and Great Shefford. His home and office is attached to the yard, and stands impressively high up, with an immediate view of the Lambourn sportsground below and much more beyond. Driving in, my eye was first caught by a series of signs warning would-be intruders of the presence of security systems, and next by a couple of small dogs which, on reflection, I could not classify as being employed to keep guard. It turned out that one belonged to the trainer, one to his head lad 'Snowy' Outen, and they were two of many such animals I was to encounter.

It is thirteen years since Hills moved into Lambourn to begin training. For nine years prior to that, he had served as head lad to a Newmarket trainer. His father had been involved in racing and, although he had been dead for some years, the passion had been passed on. 'I grew up with ponies,' recalled Barry, 'and, like most people who end up in racing, I would always rather ride than go to school. I don't think it did me any harm.'

Hills had his first ride at the Birmingham track, long since closed, in 1950. He was thirteen. By no stretch of the imagination was his career as a jockey a raging success, for he had only nine winners as an apprentice. But he was, it seemed, always destined for another department of the racing industry, and found his niche with ample time to spare.

'I am forty-four years old now,' he said as we sat in the sinking comfort of his armchairs, 'and I don't intend to do this job until I drop. I shall pack up in my early fifties, while there is still time to enjoy something else.'

Hills has the kind of face which often looks stern and harassed, yet can be transformed to relaxation in a matter of moments. One is given the impression that he has come perfectly to terms with his existence, worked out the pros and cons, and accepted his lot as not being the worst he might have ended up with. He owns ninety acres around his house, plus his own gallops. He employs between sixty and seventy full-time staff, of whom all but the two secretaries, downsman, gardener and domestic help are working in the yard. His annual wage bill is in excess of £300,000. That figure, I assumed, included a sizeable chunk to his retained jockey, Steve Cauthen, who arrived in England in 1979 heralded as the Yankee wonder boy. Now, at twenty-one, he was just beginning to come to terms with the differences in British racing and British jockeyship. 1981 had been his best season, just a handful short of a hundred winners – although maybe to him that

seemed peanuts compared with the 487 winners he partnered in the States in their 1977 season.

Hills gambled with Cauthen. Now he says it was no real
risk as the boy obviously had talent. But, just for a time –
to outsiders at least – it seemed that The Kid would not
make the transformation, that the Atlantic was too big an
ocean to cross. It was only during 1981 that matters were
put straight in everybody's mind. The diminutive Steve
from Kentucky had grown to enjoy Lambourn life. He
inhabited the local pubs, if only for his soft drinks, and
he became a popular figure around the village. 'I like it
here,' he said to me one Sunday afternoon just before the
season closed. 'This place has atmosphere, and I intend to
keep coming back, because I aim to be champion jockey.'

All of which was balm to the ears of Barry Hills, even if
he had heard it a dozen times before. He too, is intensely
ambitious, had enjoyed his best season in 1981 but was
thirsting for more. The winter, however, stretched ahead
as a barrier – even if he did intend to enjoy it.

'The routine does not change enormously between
winter and summer, in that all of the horses are still taken
out every day. They only go on the roads in the winter,
rather than on the gallops. Jumping trainers can turn their
horses away for a few months out of season, but we could
hardly do that in the freezing weather, and it would be like
locking them up in jail to leave them in their boxes for
weeks on end.

'I still get up at seven each morning. In the summer, it's
earlier – we are often on the gallops before that time – but
even when there is snow on the ground, there are always
things to attend to. My mind never really leaves the yard. I
never relax. Even when I'm away, at sales or – very
occasionally – on holiday, I phone up four times a day to
check that all is well.

'I go hunting twice a week in winter, but my main
interest is in the yearlings, of which I have bought
twenty-four this year and bred around thirty. They are

like rookie soldiers – they need to be taught manners, and I find it generally pretty satisfying to do that.'

Barry took me out through his office, where he paused to sort out another knotty problem with one of his staff. Then we wandered up two small flights of stone steps to his stable boxes, and 'Snowy' appeared, a muffled, wizened figure in a flat cap, to give the most succinct summary of Lambourn life I had yet heard. 'There's more goes on here than in the East End of London,' he said. 'We've had everything over the years, from dope to sex and from sex to . . . anything. It's the type of place where you can have £200 in your pocket one day and 200p the next – and I'm just the same as all the rest.'

'Snowy' had been with Barry Hills since he started training, as had most of his staff. Hills was plainly proud of his team, proud of his horses and proud of his village. 'It's a good community. There is little industry other than racing, but because of that the majority of people have something in common. You also find that we all know each other. I have always used the same shops and traders in the village, and I expect I always shall.'

Barry lives with his second wife, Elizabeth, and his youngest son Charles. 'He's three, and he will soon have a pony to ride.' His three elder sons, Jonathan, Michael and Richard, all ride, so the family tradition is in no danger of collapsing.

He went into flat racing for hard, financial reasons – 'there is simply no money in jumpers so I have seldom had any' – and has clearly not done badly out of his decision. But he still felt some affinity with the jumping season now unfolding around him. 'I go to National Hunt meetings now and again, and follow the results. Some of my closest friends are involved, including Nicky Henderson who is probably my best pal, and I would not miss the Cheltenham Festival for anything . . . mainly for social reasons, though.'

Socially, Barry Hills falls into the pattern of several

other Lambourn trainers. He visits the Swan in Great Shefford with some regularity, and drops into one of the village pubs 'for half a pint at eleven in the morning if I'm a bit thirsty'.

For him, the winter stretched rather shapelessly ahead. While most other racing folk in Lambourn were into what they would call 'proper' racing, Barry Hills, Peter Walwyn and associates were kicking their heels. But not really. 'It is a long winter with just the basic business, keeping the horses well and being paid for it. But still there are problems to cope with, you know. It is rather like running a hospital. There is always some emergency.'

Barry Hills stubbed out his cigar and I rose to go. His parting shot was an apt summary of his rewardingly, precarious existence. 'Training,' he said seriously, 'is hours of agony and moments of glory.'

Britain's champion jump jockey answered my knock with a yelled reply which betrayed both his Wiltshire up-bringing and his customary good humour. Despite the distressing facts that his model wife Miriam was away working in London, he had woken at six, instead of seven, for the third successive morning since the clocks went back, and he was still nursing the bruises from a most unpleasant fall nine days earlier, John Francome emerged from his side door with a cheery grin and manner which suggested he was off on his holidays rather than ready to clock in for another day's work.

He put on a check jacket over his black polo-neck sweater, said a noisy goodbye to his cat and ran a hand through his fashionably long, curly hair. Today was Wednesday, so it had to be Ascot. Francome's new Renault was in the open garage, the mud caking the sides but not quite camouflaging his own name, signwritten along the door. It was a new toy for Francome. A month earlier, in a newspaper interview which touched on commercialism, he had happened to mention the quite astonishing fact that he did not have the fundamental benefit of a sponsored car, something many garages clammer to give to far less deserving cases from other sports. Within twenty-four hours, his local Renault dealer had been on the phone offering a car. The power of the Press . . .

Francome's fat cigar, which he puffed only briefly before parking it in the ashtray, evoked thoughts of Lester Piggott. There are parallels, too, in the cheek and coolness of their respective riding styles. But their personalities are poles apart. While Piggott is renowned for his silences, his deadpan features and his occasional dry wit, Francome is a leader among jump jockeys in more ways than mere winners. A splendidly eloquent spokesman in his fruity accent, an orchestrator of dressing-room pranks and bawdy humour, Francome is also living, bubbling proof of what can be achieved by combining artistic riding skill with a will for physical slog and a shrewd eye for the future. Witness, his home: a mansion, no less, it stands proudly atop a hill at the Wantage end of the village, with the apt name of Windyridge. Constructed of Cotswold-style stone, it connects impressively by way of driveways with a block of stable-boxes and an indoor riding school, neatly set off by stone archways. The whole thing took seven years to build, and Francome did most of the navvying with his own priceless hands.

Landowner he may be, but pompous he certainly is not. Friendly and approachable to a degree both striking and refreshing in these days when sport, hard cash and hard faces have become regrettably intertwined, John Francome is one of those people who seems either not to know, or not to want to know, how good he is at his chosen profession.

By the time he reached his twenty-ninth birthday in December of 1981, he was forging ahead of the pack of challenging jockeys and virtually unbackable favourite for his fourth championship, the hardest-won prize in sport. There is no pampering, no frills and precious few luxuries in the existence of the National Hunt jockey. Just ten months every year of touring the country, risking limb if not life and taking the kicks and bruises without tantrums. In the 1980–81 season Francome had 574 rides, of which 105 were winners, 77 finished second and 63 third. The rest were unplaced and about one in ten of the total would have ended up on the floor with Francome, in the practised, instinctive way of all natural jockeys, rolling rapidly out of the flying hooves.

To an outsider, even an interested observer, it often seems a lunatic way to earn a living. There have been some who lost their nerve, a few who even admitted it and got out while the going was good. Others, more tragic, who never knew when to give up and still have the scars as testimony to their courage, devotion or madness. John Francome has always insisted that he would know when to stop, and I believe him. He has the unusual gift of being able to take a detached view of racing and of his part in it, but any who mistake his attitude as being frivolous or capricious might be treated to a rare sharp end of the Francome tongue. 'All this stuff about me not caring has begun to get up my nose,' he says in answer. 'Besides taking the overall title three times, I've been the leading jockey in the south for the past seven years, and I want it to stay that way.'

Francome is retained by Fred Winter, who has in recent years been the most consistently successful trainer in England. His rivalry with the veteran Fulke Walwyn, whose training headquarters are just the other side of a wall, is legend in Lambourn. Both are wise old heads; both recognize Francome as currently the best in the business. Winter says it protectively, Walwyn perhaps a little enviously. But they both mean it.

Unlike most jockeys, who join stables from school and graduate after doing their time as lads, Francome came into the game from the other end of the equine sports. He was a junior champion showjumper and the riding style which marked his youth still sets him apart from the crowd now. When he switched to racing – straight to National Hunt, as he was always too heavy for the flat – it was to Winter's yard at Uplands, where he has stayed ever since.

Their relationship is based on mutual respect. Trite but true. Like any other employee, from shop floor to board-room, Francome cracks the odd joke about his guv'nor. He also mutters the odd complaint. But when challenged for his opinions on Mr Winter, he calls him, 'The best trainer anyone could ever hope to ride for. He under-stands the game so totally, and what is more important, he is completely fair and very loyal to his riders. There are some trainers who will make the jockey their scapegoat for defeat if an owner is upset. But our guv'nor will never do that. I reckon we've only had two fall-outs in ten years and they were soon forgotten.'

As we set off for Ascot on that late October morning, this engaging son of a builder chatted about every subject outside racing. Of that, he would soon have his fill. 'At this time of year the season sometimes seems to stretch end-lessly ahead. I'm not saying I don't enjoy it – but all I seem to have time for, once the real racing gets underway, is driving, riding and sleeping.'

So we avoided too much discussion of his four fancied rides that day, or of the fifty thousand miles he would undoubtedly put on the clock of his sponsored car by the start of the next June, or his least favourite topic – the incessant self-deprivation to keep to an even reasonable riding weight. It pained John even to think about it; after all, he not only enjoyed eating well, he was even part-owner of a fish-and-chip shop in Swindon. We talked instead of soccer, from the silky skills of the wayward genius Maradona to the honest effort of Francome himself in a five-a-side indoor match involving a number of other jockeys the previous Sunday. We talked of tennis, his favourite sporting relaxation, and of motor-racing, which clearly lured him rather more than the slower, four-legged variety at that particular moment, and rock records and concerts, of which he is a devotee, current films and even motorway maintenance. They all provided talking points down the M4, and along the A329 to the first jump meeting of the winter at the course more famous for picnic lunches and outrageous hats than Wellington boots and sheepskins. Even when we drove into the car park, there was no tension in Francome. He would depart for another weighing-room prank, another nerveless text-book ride.

But something, just a little something, was preying on his mind. For the first time in a few years, there was a new, southern challenger for his coveted title. His name was Scudamore, son of a famous father and possessor of an almost obsessive desire to be a champion jockey. Peter Scudamore had been threatening to push Francome last season, until a cracked skull in the first week of May decided it all rather unsatisfactorily. Now a good year older, he was looking a good year better. For those who still, despite all the contrary evidence, doubted Francome's commitment to success, this was to be an acid test.

2·In Days Gone by . . .

SEATED at his desk in the front window of his bungalow on Hungerford Hill, John Rodbourn has a sweeping view down Lambourn's main street towards the square. Although he has been in the bungalow only two years, since his retirement, he knows every inch of that view and virtually, indeed, every inch of Lambourn, where he has lived all of his sixty-eight years.

There are few better-known families in the village than the Rodbourns, and for good reason. For three generations, spanning 125 years, they acted as Lambourn correspondent for the Press Association racing desk, which ostensibly entailed reporting the gallops of the local horses and supplying the agency with names of jockeys. In reality, as I found out, it involved a great deal more.

In the days of Harry, John's father, and most certainly of Henry, his grandfather, many trainers did not take kindly to the men whose job it was to disclose the form and fitness of each horse to eager punters through their morning newspaper. The trainers' view was that such preparatory exercises as gallops and schooling should be for the eyes of themselves, their jockeys and owners only, for these were the days when mornings on the downs really did act as trials for races, with a trainer only assessing his horses' chances through their galloping work rather than the race-form of their opponents. So the trainers would do all in their power to avoid being observed, while the correspondent, like any good journalist, would determine not to miss a single significant gallop. The result of this difference of opinion was a number of years in which the incumbent Rodbourn could at various stages be detected behaving like an undercover spy from a James Bond film.

By the time John, the last in the line of Lambourn racing correspondents, took over the duties from his father in 1948, rather friendlier relations prevailed, flourishing to the point when, at John's retirement, the local trainers organized a secret party for him at the home of Peter Walwyn. 'Peter had phoned to ask my wife and me round for a drink,' recalls this man with the deceptively solemn features. 'It was a Friday lunchtime, so I assumed it would be a quick glass of something as they would be going racing. But when we got there, I knew different. Cars were parked everywhere, and someone asked me when the presentation was being made. That let out the secret, but it was a marvellous day. It happened to be the day on which Steve Cauthen arrived in the village from America to ride for Barry Hills. He was brought straight down to the party and I was introduced to him. He was a nice lad, although I wondered if he thought we were a drunken lot in Lambourn!'

John crossed the floor of his lounge to lift a silver tray off the sideboard. It was inscribed, a retirement gift from various friendly and grateful trainers – yes, by that time, trainers were actually grateful for the Rodbourn services. He can remember the hostile times plainly, however, and proceeded to tell me about them.

Grandfather Henry began his racing career as a jockey, attached to Joseph Saxon, the original trainer at the yard now occupied with such distinction by Fulke Walwyn. But in 1845, doctors advised Henry Rodbourn to retire from riding; otherwise, they warned, he might be dead within six months through dangerous wasting. The caution heeded, Henry quit, and started life again as the correspondent for Lambourn.

Details of his formative years in the reporting job are, naturally, hazy, but much more is known of the period between the wars when Harry Rodbourn was in charge. Stories of his clandestine operations on the downs have been passed down the years and now form part of Lambourn legend.

He worked with a telescope, which John still keeps among his proudest possessions. The horses were picked out at a distance, and notes made on their running. Sometimes, if the trainer wished to be secretive and Harry did not, he would dress in a shepherd's smock, take out a stick and go out among the sheep, close enough to the gallops to observe everything which occurred but perfectly disguised.

'On one occasion,' John recalls, 'father spent three days and three nights on the downs, waiting for Indian Queen's last gallop before the Cambridgeshire. He dared not come home for fear of missing it. Eventually, he saw it and reported it, of course. I doubt whether the trainer was pleased – they seldom were.'

One trainer, indeed, was so incensed that his horses' work had been reported that he threatened Harry with a shotgun. Another apparently took it even harder, went out on to the downs and slit his own throat. The friendly local journalist was anything but the most popular man in the village, it seems.

There were no four-day declarations in those days and punters never knew the runners until shortly before the race was off, so the trainer's little deceptions did not end on the downs. John Rodbourn relates that his father's brother was in the village one morning when he saw Song of Essex, a highly-rated horse trained by Hugh Nugent, being led up the hill to its stable with a bandaged leg. The horse was due to run at Cheltenham that afternoon, but when the lad leading him was quizzed, he reported that he was lame and could not go to post. Harry Rodbourn was told by his brother, and a wire was immediately dispatched from the post office to catch the midday editions of the evening papers, revealing that the highly-fancied

Song of Essex would not run. But it was all a front; the bandages came off, the horse ran and won, no doubt at a rewarding price for its connections.

Harry Rodbourn was clearly a conscientious worker and when, one evening at six o'clock, he noticed some odd goings-on as he walked back to his house in the village centre, he investigated. Darkness was not long away, but Harry had seen some jockeys, dressed in their silks – as was the custom even for riding work at that time – and emerging from a well-known yard. He followed at a discreet distance, took notes on the twilight gallops which ensued, and then rushed back to the post office to file his report. It appeared in the following morning's *Sporting Life* and the trainer concerned was beside himself with fury. He demanded to know from Harry which member of his stable staff had passed on the information. Only by careful and patient explanation that such a tip would have been impossible, because the post office would have been closed before he had time to file, did Harry convince the angry trainer that he did not have treason on his hands.

'It would not be true or fair to make out that everyone was hostile to us in our job,' says John. 'Many trainers, even then, realized that the service could be of benefit to them, and my father made a lot of very good friends among them and their owners. He often told the story of being up on the gallops one day and meeting Lord Rothschild, who was there to watch a horse of his work. Before they parted, Lord Rothschild slipped a half-crown to father and told him to buy a drink with it!'

Had he wanted a drink, Harry Rodbourn would have experienced no difficulty in finding someone willing to dispense it. The pubs of Lambourn seldom closed, I am told, opening their doors in the early morning and remaining ready for business through to late at night.

It was in the 1930s that some enterprising director decided to make a film about the life of a top racehorse and to shoot it on location in Lambourn. The film was called

Lucky Blaze and among the local characters featured was Harry Rodbourn, playing himself. John still has a copy of the programme for the film, which pictures Rodbourn senior in typical pose, telescope to his eye, notebook poised. 'Lambourn only had a travelling cinema,' recalls John, 'and most of us had to go to Newbury to see the film. It was quite an event for the village.'

In truth, not much has happened in Lambourn in this century without one or other of the Rodbourns prominent somewhere. Harry is dead now – the mourners at his funeral read like a *Who's Who* of racing, and more than fifty wreaths were laid – and it is his son, who bears more than a passing resemblance to Denis Thatcher, who presides over the family business.

John Rodbourn was one of fifteen children. Three died very young, the survivors being six boys and six girls. The family was not affluent, by modern standards, and when John took a job as an apprentice draughtsman in Slough at the age of fourteen, his father quickly found that he could not afford to subsidize his digs. So that career was short-lived; John came home to help Harry on the downs, and has never regretted it. Encouraged by his father, John helped various local trainers with their secretarial work in the late 1930s. When war broke out, he was called up into the Army. 'But I never left England. I was posted to Catterick camp in Yorkshire, as a clerk. I served five years and eight months there and never really saw any action, nor particularly wanted to.' He would often walk or hitch lifts to the nearby race meetings during the war years, but it was a meeting of a different kind which was to have the greatest effect on his future life. A young Scottish corporal named Margaret was transferred from North Wales to work at Catterick, met John and became his wife.

In 1948, Harry Rodbourn retired and John took on the business in partnership with his brother, Cliff. They worked together for twenty-eight years until, with the changing ways of the media, there was no longer enough for two people to do. Cliff then went his own way to join a bookmaking business, leaving John to carry the job through to his retirement. Since then, nobody has succeeded him on anything like a similar basis.

'It was a seven-days-a-week job. Sundays were as busy as any other day, because the trainers were planning their runners and riders for the week ahead. You never really knew when you had finished, and at really hectic times of year the phone would ring constantly through the afternoon with trainers asking for the runners in various races. In those twenty-eight years with Cliff, I had only one holiday.'

The routine of the job sounds simple enough. Each morning, before 7.30 and often considerably earlier, John and Cliff took their places on the downs to watch the gallops. One used the telescope, identifying the horses at work, while the other took notes. In this way, John claims, he came to know by sight every single horse trained in Lambourn. 'People tell me all horses look the same, but that is just not true. Every one of them has some distinguishing mark, and in my job you had to know and recognize them immediately if you were to survive. You would pretty soon upset people if you reported a gallop by the wrong horse.

'There were times when it was very difficult to get close to the gallops, and we might not be sure of a certain horse. Then, we would normally ask one of the lads in the stable concerned, and more often than not it would turn out to be a new horse we had not seen before anyway. Another one to study and memorize.'

By lunchtime each day, the Rodbourns were back at home, manning the telephone. 'We were given the runners for the following day at midday, and part of our job was to find out the jockeys for each horse from our district.'

Such close contact with the trainers inevitably brought John a wealth of inside information you might imagine to be ideal gambling ammunition. But such was not always the case. 'There were certain trainers blindly convinced that every horse they entered would win. Those were the tips to ignore. Other trainers would only give you the nod occasionally, and sometimes I came out quite well.'

Although his official duties concerned only racing, John was occasionally called upon by the Press Association for other stories of local interest. The most major, and certainly the most vivid in his sharp memory, is the tanker disaster of the mid 1950s.

'I was coming out of a shop in the village after buying some tobacco,' he recalls, 'when I saw this tanker careering down the hill, plainly out of control. I jumped back into the doorway and it passed within a foot or so of me. It went straight across the square, pulled down some buildings on the far side and came to rest in a burst of flames. The burning fuel from the truck poured down the street into the brook, and even the water was alight at one point.'

Keeping an alert and professional outlook many full-time hacks would envy, John ran into the chemist's shop. 'I knew they sold cameras. I asked the man behind the counter if he knew how to use one, then told him to load it with film and start snapping. He was a bit reluctant, but I persuaded him. He took a whole film, and I got the pictures on the three o'clock train to Newbury. The PA had arranged to meet the train when it got to Paddington, and they appeared in the following morning's papers.'

Only one person, the truck driver, died, in what was apparently a horrifying spectacle. 'I got home shaking and pale,' relates John Rodbourn. 'Margaret had to sit me down and give me a brandy. I had not often touched the stuff at that hour of the day.'

One of the most surprising aspects of John Rodbourn's job is that he seldom attended race meetings. 'It was normally impossible to leave the phone at that time. Now and again, one of the trainers would phone up and offer to take me racing, and Cliff would be left to cope. But that was very rare.' He still goes very infrequently now, although his retirement is anything but idle.

When I called early one January afternoon, he was not back from one of his weekly duties – ferrying the old and infirm of the village to the British Legion club, of which he is vice-chairman and a founder member. He has also spent many years on the parochial Church Council, and bemoans the falling congregations at the attractive church in the village square. Margaret, for good measure, belongs to the Women's Institute, a local choir and the Meals-on-Wheels organization, so to see both Rodbourns sitting lazily in their front-room armchairs is an improbable sight.

But racing is still flowing freely in John's blood. He is one of the country's most knowledgeable authorities on past races, and when he and Margaret moved to their bungalow from the large family house down in the village, one of his most pressing problems was to accommodate the mountain of form books stretching back more than fifty years. He has been able to solve the most obscure questions on breeding and form from friends and acquaintances and, although he may quietly grumble about the time it takes him, loves every minute.

Lambourn has now found the perfect way to keep John Rodbourn usefully employed. It was the idea of Barry Hills to establish a central office for race entries from the village and surrounds. He approached John to ask if he would co-ordinate the operation from home. John agreed. 'I don't know why I say yes to these things,' he says with mock gloom. But he is delighted to be involved.

Every Tuesday morning now, more than thirty trainers come personally, or send their representatives, to the bungalow with entries for a forthcoming week of meetings. John collects them all, and one of Barry Hills' staff completes the courier operation by driving them up to Weatherby's office in Wellingborough. Then on Wednesday afternoon, the racing calendars arrive, with the entries printed in race programme order. It is John's job to distribute them, and he does most of the Lambourn trainers himself, on foot.

Most mornings, John can sit in that front window of his and watch the strings of horses pass on the road outside. Riders wave to him, trainers stop to chat. The tall bespectacled, grey-haired figure is known by all and, despite the controversial history of the Rodbourn family, liked unanimously.

In a green sweater and a pair of striking plus-fours, a cigarette constantly at hand as he chattily reminisced in a brogue sometimes difficult to pick up, Freddie Maxwell looked the epitome of an Irish country gentleman. Which, I suppose, is just what he is.

It was in Ireland, the town of Birr to be precise, that Freddie was born, raised and educated into the ways of the racing world. But like many others of his background and generation, he came to England. He lived in Lambourn for an initial five-year spell before the war and returned in 1957. He has lived there ever since, and now holds court in a house on the hill called Folly Road, where he moved on retiring from training in 1979.

John Francome, pointing me in the direction of some village characters during the planning stages of this book, virtually insisted that Freddie Maxwell topped my list. 'He is the king of Lambourn,' he said; I could see now what he meant.

Most fine days, Freddie can be found in the impeccably neat garden he tends with almost fanatical care. He has big plans for his garden, and will discuss them in as much detail as you like. 'If you ever write a book on gardening,' he says mischievously, 'then I'm your man.'

I discovered that despite oft-repeated self-deprecation to the effect that he knew relatively little about Lambourn and its inhabitants, this dapper little man with impressive grey sideburns was also a fund of information on the village he has made his home. Interesting, too, was the disclosure that there is mutual admiration between Maxwell and Francome. Of the new riding king of the village, Freddie says unreservedly: 'He is the best jockey I have ever seen.' And his wife Nora, who comes from Yorkshire and is another of the local ladies running the Meals-on-Wheels service, adds: 'He is also a great charmer in a cheeky sort of way.'

Any judgements made by Freddie Maxwell have to be respected. He is, after all, seventy-six and one of the most senior statesmen of the village's racing fraternity. His house has a wide sweep of a drive outside and is cosily comfortable within. The sitting room wall is virtually groaning under the weight of racing prints, and the shelves are full of books on great horses and great riders. Freddie sits back in his favourite armchair, a midday glass of whisky by his side, and volubly bemoans the fact that 'I have never found a drink I like'. Prompted by his friend and near-contemporary John Rodbourn, whom he had summoned specifically for the purpose, Freddie related yarns from the past at a rate impossible to follow. Before coming to Lambourn, Freddie trained at Blewbury, the lovely village on the north-eastern edge of the same stretch of Berkshire and Oxford Downs on which Lambourn stands. He remembers that in those bygone days, Letcombe Regis, just to the north of Lambourn, was reckoned to be much more of a training centre. My questions sometimes lost a little in the transmission, and Freddie apologetically explained the reason. 'I was in the RAF in the war,' he said. 'Instructing gunners to shoot pigeons, you know, and it destroyed my ears. I've not heard properly ever since.'

His memories of the Berkshire area stretch back half a century, to the days when he worked as a lad in one of the yards which were then housed in the village of Wroughton. Freddie earned twenty-five shillings a week and tells of his dismay when King of Clubs, one of the horses he 'did', was taken away from the yard and moved to Harry Cottrell's Lambourn stables. 'We had no horse-boxes at that time, so I had to ride the horse to the Shepherd's Rest pub, which was about half-way, then a lad from Cottrell's met me and rode him the rest of the way. That was the way many moves were done in those days.'

Maxwell remembers vividly the railway line which linked Lambourn with Newbury and hence London and the south, and gave the trainers their lifeline to many of the major racecourses. 'The horses all travelled to racing by train, in special horse-box carriages,' he recalls. And John Rodbourn put in the fact that his mother had the distinction of travelling on the first and the last trains to leave the Lambourn station, which closed after a relatively short life in 1960.

There is a camouflaged sense of pride apparent in Freddie when you try to talk to him of his own achievements. 'Oh, I never did that much,' he will repeat. But others know different, especially John Rodbourn, who could look up all the winners he turned out, given an afternoon in the company of his treasured form books.

Within the village, stories abound of the gentle Irishman known to all as 'Maxie'. One of the best was related to me by his fellow countryman, the vet Frank Mahon, and concerns a day in Ireland during Freddie's riding career.

'Maxie was down to ride in a Maiden Novices Selling Chase, which must be the lowest of the low,' Frank said. 'It was a rural two-bit track, near where he lived in fact, and there was the usual stack of entries for the race. As the jockeys were circling on their mounts at the post, waiting for the starter to go on to his rostrum, the local vicar was leaning on the rails. When Maxie passed, he called out, "I've not seen you in church lately." The horses circled again, and the next time Freddie was within earshot, the vicar shouted: "Why have you not been coming to church to pray?" Maxie had said nothing during all this, but now spun towards the vicar and yelled back: "If you'd ever ridden in a Maiden Novices Selling Chase, you would realize I can say enough prayers before we jump the first to make up for any amount of missed Sundays!" '

3·Dawn on the Downs

LAMBOURN'S twilight world is hectic. Each morning during the winter, come fog, frost or snow, lights flick on around the village before seven, and hunched, furtive-looking figures scurry busily across yards of stone or gravel carrying bowls of corn-feed and muttering no more than curt and fruity greetings to the horses. The dawn ritual has been observed for decades past, but this makes it no less fascinating to the newcomer. On 20 November, all the ingredients were right. The dying night had been bleak and stormy and the new day was grumbling like a hangover. Rain danced on the windscreen of my car as I drove slowly among the twinkling lights of Upper Lambourn and a fierce wind rattled the broken wooden gates of Nick Gaselee's yard as I turned in at precisely 7.25.

Nicholas Auriol Gaselee was two months short of his forty-third birthday and eight days short of having a pot at the Hennessy Gold Cup with Doddington Park, the best horse to come under his wing in his five years as a trainer. But Doddington's preparation for this, the first of the season's most desirable prizes, had suffered a major setback when he was brought down at Cheltenham a week earlier. Although sound enough physically, Gaselee feared that confidence had been drained, and this morning had been set aside for a session of recuperative schooling over the fences on the downs.

The trainer was already supervising affairs when I arrived. He was strolling around the yard, brandishing a stick of intimidating appearance and issuing the occasional instruction to one or other of his lads as they hurried to get their individual horses ready for the morning gallops. He greeted me politely, then parked me somewhere unobtrusive while his directions continued apace.

'Where on earth is Richard?' he said rhetorically, and no sooner were the words out than the splash of tyres in a puddle announced the arrival of a Ford Escort driven by Richard Linley. He looked a little harassed and just a touch bleary. The drive from his home in the village of Zeals, a few miles east of Wincanton racecourse, had taken only minutes over the hour but had necessitated leaving his bed before six. It was the same every Tuesday and Friday, the usual days when he would drive up to Lambourn to school horses for Gaselee.

'You ride Doddington, Richard,' were the four words issued by trainer to jockey as Linley scrambled out of his car, already clad in anorak and breeches and pulling on his helmet as he trotted through the haybarn to the box housing the Hennessy hope.

It was 7.42 as the first of Gaselee's string filed out of the yard, turning left along a narrow lane and then right up a bridle path to the downs. Nick beckoned me into the passenger seat of his Land-Rover and we followed the horses out.

Nick Gaselee is a large man with a faintly aristocratic face and greying hair. He has only to speak to reveal his own good breeding and, watching him stride around with his stick, it was possible to imagine him in his previous life as an army regular. He served in such far-flung spots as Muscat and the Oman. 'We were there just as the oil was found; it was very active and exciting, real soldiering, and I loved the place.' Then he did a spell at Knightsbridge Barracks in London. 'That was very different, but equally enjoyable. I might have considered a long career in the army, but when I was twenty-four they sent me to Bovingdon on a driving and maintenance course. I don't know if they were trying to tell me something, but it was a clear enough message to me. I decided I had seen enough of forces life.'

When Gaselee left the army he had already decided that he wanted to ride. This he did with some distinction, riding ninety winners over jumps as an amateur, chiefly while based at Newmarket. He flirted briefly with a life in Lambourn, but left again to become racing correspondent of the *Evening Standard*. Journalism was never destined to be his long-term future, however, and by 1971 he was ensconced once more in Lambourn as assistant to the man who plainly became his mentor, Fulke Walwyn.

Five years in the charge of the maestro was an impeccable graduation course, and Gaselee took out a licence of his own in 1976. His list of owners now is impressive in length and quality; many of the names can be found in *Who's Who*. Successes have been steady though unspectacular, and if Doddington landed the Hennessy it would be the biggest honour to come the trainer's way.

We disembarked from the Land-Rover on the edge of the schooling ground and Nick surveyed the scene like a mariner looking out on a stormy sea. The downs was no place for faint hearts and fevers that morning. A gale howled, rain still blew bitingly into our faces. I felt cold and damp but invigorated. As I watched the downsmen at work, I wondered at their hardiness; this was a mild morning compared to many they would face that winter.

The Gaselee horses were first on the schooling grounds. As usual, he had phoned in advance to warn Eddie Fisher, the foreman of the downsmen, of his intentions. Doddington Park jumped the series of fences twice, Gaselee discussing each effort with Linley. They agreed that he was not as fluent as he might be and would need another morning of schooling before the race.

Two of Gaselee's hurdlers were next to be schooled, and Linley hurriedly changed horses. Nick was more relaxed now, and talked of his job as we watched. 'There are days,' he conceded, 'when you don't want to get up at the crack of dawn again . . . I suppose to a large extent it's dependent on the previous night . . . but I feel I am lucky to be doing something I love and, generally speaking, to be doing it from home. I have forty horses in the yard now – there are some comings and goings, but I could not take many more anyway – and they are all like children to me. Like any other trainer, I develop a greater affection for certain of my horses, but I am just as concerned about the rest. I worry, too. I probably should enjoy a holiday each year, but I have ten days away in the summer and that's it. I'm very bad at going away and leaving the horses.'

It was clear that Gaselee's liking for the job extended beyond an affinity with horses. He relished the way of life, and above all the countryside in which he found himself operating. As we drove back to the yard, leaving behind a steadily growing band of Lambourn trainers, jockeys, lads and horses on the downs, he pointed out landmarks with genuine enthusiasm. He talked too, of his own staff – of head lad 'Jumbo' Heaney who had been with him since he began training, and of the soccer, darts and tug-of-war competitions in which his lads had been involved. 'I gave them moral support only, in the tug-of-war,' he smiled.

We descended the track and turned back into the lane towards his stables. 'Other parts of the village have changed,' he said. 'Estates have been built, and many of the people there have no interest in racing at all. But this part, in Upper Lambourn, is just as it was years ago, quite unspoiled. I love it here.'

Unlike most trainers, Gaselee does not live on site. His cottage is a short walk around the corner and down one of Upper Lambourn's warren of lanes diving off the Shrivenham Road. Inside, it was all I would have expected – a farmhouse-style kitchen, open plan, an office on the left of the entrance porch and a phone which began ringing on cue as the teapot was produced.

Judith Gaselee has been married to Nick for fifteen years, since before the training days were more than a pipe-dream, and knows the breakfast score backwards. Nick has egg, bacon, sausage and tomato, plus tea, but it is invariably eaten cold after he has answered the umpteenth call or finished studying the entries in the *Sporting Life* which lay on the table as we entered.

The kitchen was something of a menagerie. Three dogs lay on an old sofa by the door, seemingly happy in each other's company. A parrot squawked cleverly in a cage above them, and his words – 'puss, puss, puss' – betrayed the fact that one of the family was missing, perhaps stalking the mouse which had, much to Judith's apparent disgust, been added to the collection in recent weeks.

The children were absent, both at boarding school. They have a son named James and a daughter Sarah Jane, who became a celebrity in the summer when she was a bridesmaid at the wedding of one of Nick's owners. The wedding was at St Paul's Cathedral and most of the country had a day off to celebrate.

Richard Linley came in and sat down with his own copy of the *Sporting Life*. His breakfast was confined to a cup of tea – two if he was lucky. Like most jump jockeys, he has a constant battle to do the minimum weight of ten stone. Exceed it, and you risk losing rides. Richard and Nick pored over the four-day declarations for Monday's meetings at Leicester and Windsor. Linley had already been asked to ride for another trainer, Peter Bailey, at the former meeting. But Gaselee was considering running one or two at Windsor, and he had first claim on Linley's services.

It was the type of scene, the type of discussion, which could have easily been played out at dozens of other trainers' breakfast tables around the country that morning. Certainly it was odds-on that conversations were following similar lines within a mile of where we were sitting. Trainer and jockey retired to the office, still chatting about Doddington Park's jumping. I retired to the loo, which I found adorned with prints and photographs, including one of a familiar figure on horseback. The inscription beneath it read: 'To the instructor, from the grateful pupil – Charles. March 1980.'

As I left, Nick was on the phone again . . . to Buckingham Palace.

Instead of making its first visit to Nick Gaselee's stable, the Hennessy Gold Cup returned to familiar territory. It was won by Diamond Edge, trained by the grand old man responsible for six previous Hennessy winners, not to mention four Cheltenham Gold Cups, six Whitbread triumphs and a single Grand National. One might have imagined that the novelty of victory had long since left Fulke Walwyn's life. But, almost a month after his seventy-first birthday, the doyen of all trainers was insisting that the tingle of excitement was as acute as when he trained his very first winner at about the time Hitler was marshalling his invasion forces.

One month before this latest success with Diamond Edge, Walwyn had saddled six runners at two meetings on a midweek afternoon, and they had all won. Age, it seemed, had neither jaded his gift of producing the right horses for the right races, nor affected the quality of his string. Most assuredly, it had not damaged his enthusiasm.

He was standing in the middle of his yard when I drove in. Like his former pupil Gaselee, he carried a heavy stick, and was amply protected against the cold of early winter by, it turned out, two thick anoraks and a bright yellow sweater with the words 'Gay George' knitted in red across the chest. This was not, I quickly realized, some improbable reference to an effeminate friend, but the name of one of Walwyn's crack hurdlers, aimed once more this year at the Champion Hurdle during Cheltenham's March Festival. 'The owners gave it to me,' explained Walwyn in his gruff, yet kindly voice. 'I wear it because he is a very good horse . . . it's also a very warm sweater.'

A slow smile crossed his comfortably ruddy face. We sat down in his office, where soft armchairs jostled for position with a large desk and upright chair. A bookcase along one wall contained a row of *Debrett's* and *Burke's Peerage*, and virtually on cue Fulke's wife Catherine entered. The daughter of Sir Humphrey de Trafford, and Mrs Walwyn for twenty-nine years, she mixed his customary lunchtime drink without needing to check the measures with him.

Fulke Walwyn was born in Monmouthshire and grew up in the Welsh border country with an army career awaiting him. His family were not involved in racing to a great degree although his uncle was father to his neighbour Peter Walwyn, almost as successful on the flat as is Fulke over jumps. Now the Walwyn family dominates the most famous of Lambourn's 32 training establishments. Peter is based at Seven Barrows, which has been producing top-class racehorses for over a century. Among the first was Bendigo, which won a series of rich flat races in the 1880s. Legend has it that the horse's trainer, Charles Joussieffe, paid for the lych-gate at Lambourn Church in memory of Bendigo's prodigious record of success.

Fulke's headquarters is Saxon House, named after Joseph Saxon who trained there around 1850. Ted Gwilt, another of the village's most famous names, was also based there before Walwyn moved in during 1944, transferring his business across the village from Delamere, now the home of Dick Francis's trainer son, Merrick. Saxon House fairly reeks of history, and of success, and Fulke looks so content and at one with the place that it comes as something of a surprise to learn that he was not born there.

He in fact enjoyed an eleven-year riding career before turning to training, and was no failure at that, either. He turned professional only after winning the National on Reynoldstown in 1936. But it is as a producer of winners, rather than a rider of them, that Fulke Walwyn will always be remembered, and he acknowledges the fact graciously, with a sage nod of his wise old head and a sackful of anecdotes.

For much of his training career, the Saxon House boxes have been filled to capacity. 'We always used to have sixty-five or seventy in,' he recalls. 'But of those, twenty would be flat horses. I gave that up a few years ago and concentrated entirely on jumping, where my heart has always been. I find I have much more affinity with the old jumping horses. Once they have been around for a few years, and won some decent races, they become household heroes. But on the flat, the average member of public has hardly got used to a horse's name when it is retired to stud, gone from the racecourses forever.'

Of the many household heroes he has trained himself, Fulke has one particular favourite. 'It isn't easy to select one horse from the hundreds, and there have been so many good ones . . . Taxidermist, Mill House, Team Spirit and the rest. But the best, I suppose, must have been Mandarin.' It is not a surprising choice, but a slightly ironical one, as Mandarin was ridden to victory in the 1962 Gold Cup by the man who has since become Fulke's neighbour and rival, Fred Winter.

Walwyn sat quietly enthusing over plans for his newest hero, Diamond Edge. 'He is good enough to win a Gold Cup. So far he has been unlucky in the race, but the course suits him and if the race and conditions go well, I have high hopes this year.'

It at no stage occurred to the man that most contemporaries of his would be quite content to sit back and enjoy their retirement, coming no nearer to thoughts of a Gold Cup winner than a possible few pounds each way on their fancy. Fundamentally, Fulke had not altered his routine over the past forty-two years, barring the solitary concession to advancing years of accompanying his string to morning exercise in his Land-Rover, rather than on horseback. 'I rode out every day until I was sixty-six,' he said in a voice which almost sheepishly regretted the five years since. 'I still get up before seven each morning. I'm woken with a cup of tea, and I make sure I'm in the yard in time to direct operations. I suppose I dislike delegating too much. I have to be involved in everything concerned with the yard. Or, at least, if I can't do it all myself, I have to see it being done. I have twenty-three on my full-time staff, and a good many of them have been with me twenty years or more. I like it that way, because the longer they have been here the better they understand me. I need that,' he added with another of those twinkling smiles which bely the initially stern impression his features can portray.

He took another draught from his glass and mused: 'Of course, I don't have late nights very often these days. That's one thing that has altered with the years. But otherwise my routine is just as it has always been . . . and I am not sure if I could cope very easily with having it changed after all this time.'

I could not resist asking why, with every conceivable honour already won, he still goes on with this exacting job.

'Because I have come to the conclusion that it is a great mistake to retire,' he replied readily. 'It is always the wives of other trainers who tell me this. Their husbands have packed up and always regretted it, so I decided to carry on until I'm not capable of doing the job. Besides, I love it so much, you see. I don't know how I would pass the time if I didn't keep at it.'

In the very week that Fulke Walwyn was celebrating six winners in a single day and convincing himself that retirement was still as far away as ever, a near neighbour, nineteen years his junior, was giving it all up.

Reg Akehurst was almost as far removed from Fulke Walwyn in measures of success as were their respective entries in the trainers' directory. But he had, nevertheless, held a licence for nineteen years, the last eleven of

41

which had been spent in the Upper Lambourn yard where he ended his career, and there had been times when as many as forty horses were in his charge. A month after announcing that he was selling up, Akehurst was talking of going abroad to live. He had planned a January trip to Portugal, to play golf, find some sun on his back and ease the arthritic aches which were his constant winter reminder of the more bruising falls during his years as a National Hunt rider. 'As soon as the weather gets cold, I start feeling the pain again,' he reported. 'I need a warm climate, and who knows, I might find a job out there and settle for good.'

But there was more to his decision than a desire to follow the sun. Akehurst had been forced out of racing by trends which were threatening every small trainer, in Lambourn and around the country. 'In my time, I have had doubles at Sandown and Goodwood, and decent winners at Ascot,' he explained as we sat in his front room looking out over the 'ghost' yard. 'But today, the same horses who won those races would struggle to win a moderate event on a Monday at Leicester. I was left behind because my owners were not prepared to pay out tens of thousands of pounds. I can't say I blame them. In fact, it got to the stage when I began to feel sorry for the owners, because I would go somewhere like Leicester with my best horses, and they would get beaten by the fourth division of Michael Stoute or Henry Cecil. I remember asking Henry once, semi-seriously, why he could not give the small trainers a chance and stay away from the moderate meetings. He answered very fairly that when you have 120 or more horses in your yard, there simply aren't enough good races and meetings to go round.'

Akehurst was not bitter. Neither did he resent the years he had spent vainly trying to build a fruitful business. He did not want to leave Lambourn, but he would, because he was a realist.

A neat man of fifty-two with a trim figure and greying hair, he had spent all his life in the south of England. Born in Folkestone, he had based himself in Ascot during his riding years, then trained at Basingstoke and Epsom in leased yards before buying the Neardown stables in Lambourn.

His wife Sheila was not only a staunch support to him in the business – 'owners like to be looked after when they come to see their horse, and Sheila has always been marvellous in that respect' – but she had her own active role in village life as owner of the Odds'n'Jods shop which sold as great a variety of clothing and riding equipment as its name suggests. She did not run it personally these days, leaving the counter in the capable hands of downs foreman Eddie Fisher's sister – everywhere in Lambourn, there are family links – but now a decision would have to be made on the future of the shop, too.

The Akehursts have two sons, Murray and Jonathan. For some years, Jonathan had been race-riding, on the flat or over jumps. He wanted to make a career out of National Hunt riding, but was finding himself faced with an overcrowded register of jockeys all clamouring for the same mounts. There were simply not enough to go round.

'I am at an age,' said Reg Akehurst, 'when I am constantly surprised by how much things cost. Maybe that was another factor in my decision to quit. I look around Lambourn, and there are many others at my level, small trainers battling against the odds by themselves. But most of them are younger than me, and they will struggle on, not seeing the wood for the trees but living on hope and enthusiasm. Eventually, though, some of them will follow me in giving up. It was not an easy decision, nor was it a hasty one. I had been in racing all my life and you can't cut yourself off without a lot of hard thinking. My luck could have changed. I could have gone blindly on, kidding myself that it would all come right. But with the economic climate as it is, I knew it never would. It's been a constant battle for me in racing, but I wouldn't knock it. I've been given a great life and I would probably do it again if I was young. But I would like to see some improvements made, the most important of which would be an increase in prize money. With the type of horses that I had – and many other trainers still have – the only way to make a decent living is by becoming a betting yard. And that can't be a healthy thing for racing.'

The horses had all gone from Neardown, distributed among other trainers. The yard was up for sale, but it remained intact and was kept sparklingly clean by the remaining staff. Reg paused at the window to stare out at the stables, once full of horses running with his name beside them on the racecard.

'I miss it,' he said. 'I can't pretend otherwise. For years, I had been used to getting up before seven and immediately busying myself with the usual trainer's round of jobs. Now, I still wake at the same time, then think to myself, What the hell is there to get up for? There seems nothing worthwhile left.'

Nine months on, Reg Akehurst accepted that his life was bound up with horses and hoped his future still lay in racing. He was going to try again.

4·Deadly White Christmas

THE bedroom in Eddie Fisher's cottage at New Barn Farm seemed colder than usual on the morning of Tuesday, 8 December. Rising, as ever, at 6.30, Eddie quickly confirmed his worst suspicions. Gazing out of his window at the path which leads quickly on to his beloved downs, he surveyed an endless carpet of white. Snow had come early this season. Not being of the type to breathe a sigh of relief and get back into bed, Eddie Fisher would have muttered a curse or two under his breath, made some tea and then set forth to try and make the best of a bad job. But the mere sight of the snow would have been enough to tell him that his normal duties, those he had performed virtually daily for twenty-six years, were quite redundant.

No face or figure is more familiar than Eddie's to the racing population of Lambourn. As downsman, responsible for the five hundred acres of gallops owned by the Nugent Estates, he commands the respect, admiration and, in certain cases even the fear, of trainers and jockeys around the village. Eddie is responsible for maintaining the gallops, and the schooling hurdles and fences, and for designating the areas to be used each morning. He does not take kindly to any disobediance, and there are few among the trainers served by the Fisher system who do not harbour some hairy tale of Eddie's temper being ignited by a misguided attempt to use different gallops, or at a different time, to those laid down. 'I like to think I'm on good terms with all of the trainers,' he says. 'But if they do anything wrong, I'm on top of them – and then the language starts. The air might be blue for a few minutes, and they get the message alright. I have to tell them, you

45

see . . . it's part of my job.'

Eddie is a ruddy-faced, well-built man with honest eyes and a healthy head of hair. Every inch of him confirms the impression that he has spent most hours of his life outdoors, and that the sight of an office or the smell of a factory would be complete anathema. He was born in Lambourn, the son of a plumber, and although his family were not directly involved in racing, his interest bloomed. An initial factory job in Hungerford, straight from school, was short-lived, and he was working on one of Dick Radbourne's Lambourn farms when the downsman job became vacant. He was nineteen when he took on the position which was to become his life's work, his pride and joy.

Eddie's routine is well-oiled and seldom changes. He is always on the schooling ground by 7.30, preparing the obstacles for the invasion of horses which he knows will start twenty minutes later. 'Most of the trainers just turn up and expect things to be ready for them. But one or two do phone in advance, to warn me and let me know which of the fences or hurdles they want to use. Mr Walwyn often phones, and Mr Gaselee always does.' Eddie, in the time-honoured racing custom of respecting people who give you a job, refers to every trainer as 'Mr'.

There are twenty-one assorted fences on the schooling ground, and three sets of variously sized hurdles. Horses will be schooled if they are new to either hurdling or chasing, or if they have recently suffered a fall, with its consequent drain on confidence.

By 9.30, the first part of the day is over. The schooling complete, Eddie and his two helpers – his brother, Stan, and a lad named Andrew Rose – stop for breakfast. It is hardly a leisurely banquet. 'Just tea and sandwiches. We're working again by a quarter to ten.'

For the remainder of the day, barring an hour's lunch-break, Eddie and his team patrol the gallops, armed with forks to replace divots as soon as horses have passed. The gallop courses are changed every day, Eddie explains with some pride, and he is reluctant to use a roller with any frequency 'because it produces false ground'. So the downsmen walk and fork. 'We pack up at 4.30, and I reckon we have generally walked nine or ten miles each by that time.'

The downsmen's busiest time of year is in March and April, when the jumping season reaches its climax at Cheltenham and Aintree and the new flat season is getting under way. 'Then it really does get hectic. I get home each night bloody exhausted,' said Eddie. 'But I like being busy. I get a real thrill each time one of our Lambourn trainers has a winner. It gives me a sense of satisfaction, as I reckon we have played some small part in preparing that horse. I don't have much time to go racing myself – the occasional trip to Newbury is about my limit – but I follow it with great interest. I want to see the horses racing all the time, you see.'

Which explains why Eddie was a mite depressed when I slithered up the anonymous-looking track, a mile out of the village, to find his cottage. It was 10 December and the snow was enjoying its third day of disruption, showing no signs of relenting. Snowy barns and frozen tractors gave the farm a ghostly aspect, and as Eddie answered the door, he cast his eyes grimly skywards. It said enough. His cottage is comfortable, lived-in. The inside of the back door has a dart board hanging on it. The floor was a busy jumble of boots. Eddie apologized for the mess and introduced me to his wife, a short, mild woman with a friendly face, who works part-time on the adjoining farm. The Fishers' dog, a four-year-old pedigree labrador bitch, roused herself briefly, stretched and showed some interest in my arrival, then sensibly settled down again next to the fire. Eddie, dressed in a Guernsey-style sweater, working trousers and, incongruously, carpet slippers, led me into a sitting-room. The walls were adorned with the almost statutory racing prints; the family shots of his three children, all at school, stood on a table.

New Barn Farm had been home for ten years. Before that, they had a house in the village, but it was a less convenient base for Eddie. 'All I have to do now is hop on the tractor, drive it up the track and I'm on the downs. It's so handy . . . but it doesn't really matter in weather like this.

'It breaks my heart to see all this snow. It strangles the village, you know, when there isn't any racing. I haven't had a horse on the gallops, or the schooling ground, since the first falls on Tuesday – and I shan't until it clears. People might think it makes my life easy, but I would much rather be working with the horses. When the weather is like this, we go to Newbury to cut birch for the obstacles – but there is not much satisfaction in it.'

Eddie retrieved some faded newspaper cuttings from a cupboard, previous articles written about himself and his job. He apologized for not thinking too clearly this morning – 'Mr Hills had a party last night, you know' – and, after we had sat and talked for an hour, he reached for his boots and set off once more into the snow, still casting baleful, resentful glares at the grey, heavy sky.

The snow had produced a similar lack of enthusiasm at the old parsonage, in the village itself. Jim Cramsie knew all too well what such conditions would do to his business. It would mean sixteen men sitting around in the rest-room at his depot, being paid to do nothing. And it would mean himself, and his other clerical staff, going through the motions of all the customary paperwork, in the clear knowledge that only a dramatic and improbable thaw could keep the fruits of their labours out of the waste-paper basket.

Cramsie operates the Lambourn Ridgeway Transport business, which is responsible for ferrying the majority of racehorses in the Berkshire and Wiltshire Downs area to and from race meetings. It is a sister company to Lambourn Engineering, and both are owned by John Nugent. Other than the more intrinsic parts of the racing industry, these companies are the biggest single sources of employment in the village.

At first glance, Jim Cramsie does not strike you as being in the right job. Relaxed by the log-fire in his kitchen while the fog closed in on the snowbound village, he was wearing a tweed jacket, striped tie and cord trousers. He had a handkerchief, blue with white spots, in his breast pocket. His hair is that distinguished shade of grey and he resembles the hero in one of those old English films, who might just turn out to be the smooth villain in the final reel. He might sell wine, pine furniture or run a country hotel. He might be the village squire. But, given twenty questions and the odd clue, the betting is still that you would not pigeon-hole him as the boss of a horse-box business.

The facts, however, are that he has done the job for nine years, in which the company has trimmed its wings from inflated overheads and considerable losses to the point where profits are being shown. Once the operators of thirty-one boxes, they now run only eighteen and employ, other than the sixteen drivers, one travelling groom, two fitters and three office staff. All of whom, as Mr Cramsie pointed out with a gentle disfavour, were being forced by this wretched weather to kick their heels and wait idly for pay-day.

An amiable nine-month-old Lurcher hound called Fagin (his half-brother, called Dodger, died recently) came forward to lick my feet and survey the fire as Jim settled down to tell me the rudiments of the transport business, whose boxes with their prominent L.R.T. logo had established the identity of the village in the minds of many people quite disinterested in racing.

The company had been formed in 1932, and expanded to the current point at which it serviced over half of the fifty-two trainers and permit-holders based between Beckhampton in the west and Blewbury in the east. In the summer, they carry around a thousand horses each month, but surprisingly – for Lambourn is known more for its National Hunt centres – the number drops to three hundred in the winter. The boxes are of varying capacities, upwards from two to nine horses, although the biggest are more often used for ferry work than for day-to-day race transport.

A telephone is manned twenty-four hours a day, 365 days a year. 'Maybe that isn't true,' concedes Jim, 'you might struggle for an answer for a couple of hours during Christmas lunchtime.' The system works through the duty officer taking the telephone home in the evening and having all calls to the business switched through to his or her number. 'You might wonder why it is necessary to have constant manning. But in fact there are a number of good reasons. The first is that we travel overnight to all meetings more than a certain distance from Lambourn. Horses are valuable, as are drivers, and on an evening like this, you don't want a box stuck in a layby somewhere on the road to Catterick, with four or five horses freezing to death inside. The drivers need a number they can phone in times of emergency.

'Similarly, practically every day of the year, one or more of our boxes will be returning to Lambourn late at night after a meeting at a far-off course. The ferries also leave late at night, and if there is any problem over the horses' paperwork, we must have someone available to sort it out.

'The other main reason is that trainers, by their very nature, often like to leave the declaring of runners until the last possible moment. They have to declare them by eleven o'clock on the morning of the day prior to the race concerned, but it is in our interests to hope that they might do it sooner. Left so late, it gives us precious little time to organize the correct-sized box and brief the driver, if the meeting requires an overnight run. So we are available to trainers if they feel like letting us know their runners any time of the day or night.'

Most of Jim Cramsie's drivers have been doing the job for a dozen years or more and grown used to the unusual demands and unpredictability of it all. 'They generally have some sort of racing background, whether by having done their time with a trainer, or dabbled as a jockey or whatever. They do need to know something about horses, to cope with all eventualities, even if they do usually have the company of the horse's lad. They obviously need to be good drivers – you can't throw these things about – and they need to be fairly phlegmatic about their programme. It's a very varied existence. They might do nothing one day, and the next they could be off to Newbury, or Cartmel, or Ireland, or even Spain. By the nature of the business, it is seldom possible to tell each driver his duties for the following day until he returns from his current job. So a driver turning back into Lambourn just before midnight will have no idea where he might be going the next morning. They complain about not knowing, but I reckon it must give them a bit more job satisfaction this way.'

The drivers' foreman is Clarence Deakin, who has been doing the job a mere thirty-five years. There are anecdotes concerning him, and virtually every other driver, but none is featured more regularly than the improbably named Mickey Flynn – an Irishman, believe it or not – who retired from the business a few years ago. A colourful character whose past included fighting in the Spanish Civil War, Mickey apparently specialized in finding short cuts home from the various racecourses. One day, with a full cargo of horses, a groom and several lads, he confidently set off down a side street informing everyone in general that this route cut miles off the journey. He was unabashed even when confronted by a brick wall directly across the road. A dead end, in fact. Mickey refused to believe that it was not possible to get through and insisted that one of the grooms shinned up the wall to see what was on the other side. 'They've built it since the last meeting here, I know that,' he insisted. The groom did as he was told, then tried hard to keep a straight face as he imparted to Mickey the news that, on the far side of the wall were a series of patently old railway sidings. Turning the box round with good grace, Mickey announced: 'That's been done since the last meeting, too.'

Shifting only long enough to make some coffee, draw the curtains over the dreadful scene outside, and restrain Fagin from actually stepping into the fire, Jim Cramsie began to tell me about himself, his upbringing and his remarkable route to his present position of well-known and much-needed businessman, living in one of Lambourn's oldest properties.

He grew up in Lambourn, the son of an Ulster-born racehorse trainer. His childhood playmates were David and John Nugent, and the well-preserved family albums we pored over featured countless shots of three mischievous looking young lads in shorts – Jim, David and John.

'I had two donkeys at home, and used to love riding them. Sometimes, I would borrow a friend's pony, too. But I was only seven when war broke out, my father joined up and we followed him around in the army for the next few years.'

Cramsie went to Marlborough School, and on leaving followed his bent for farming and spent two years at the Agricultural College in Cirencester. He helped his uncle on a farm in Kent and worked on two more farms, but was resigned to spending two years in the army on compulsory National Service, so attempted nothing more permanent. 'My father insisted I went into the Irish guards. I had two interviews in London with fairly vicious colonels, and then failed the medical. I asked them if I was likely to be needed at any future date, and they said they would only want me in a dire national emergency. I can only assume there has not been one since!'

It was December 1956 when Cramsie set off for Australia with £15 in his pocket, and luggage consisting of four bulls, a cow and a calf, two goats, four dogs and a Siamese cat. After six weeks on board ship, this strange cargo was delivered to various destinations along the Australian coast, and Jim spent the next two years in New South Wales.

His employment during that time mostly meant riding a horse. 'The Australians asked me if I could ride, and they thought it was the funniest thing they had every heard when I told them that I did have a couple of donkeys as a boy . . . But it was just like riding a bike. I never thought of falling off, and at lunchtime I just jumped off and tied the horse up to a tree. It was all so much more free and easy there. The horses got hurt, quite badly occasionally, but everybody managed with quite basic treatment. There was never any panic about ringing for a vet.'

After a spell as a sheep-shearer – 'backbreaking; I've never drunk so much beer in my life' – Jim set off home. The journey back took him seven months, four of which were spent on a tobacco farm in Rhodesia. He travelled the last leg by train from Barcelona and arrived back at Liverpool station with a half-crown and two sixpences. 'I had been away two years and travelled all round the world. I worked out it had cost me £14 6s. 6d.

'There were a number of options when I returned to work in England, not all of them very palatable. This job came up through my connections with the Nugents, and as I wanted, at heart, to live in Lambourn, it seemed the best available choice. Funnily enough, although I have secret dreams of having a stud if ever I am very rich, it never entered my head to follow my father and train.'

All of which led on to one of Lambourn's most vivid characters, Randal Cramsie. He trained in the village before the First World War and between the wars. Only when he returned again, in 1945, did he call it a day. 'I don't think he had the stomach to start everything for a third time,' explains his son, 'so he helped Tom Rimell at his yard in Worcestershire.'

But before those years, Randal Cramsie was clearly the type of personality on which Lambourn folklore is built. In the early twenties, for instance, he made it his business to create an improvement in the local fire service, which had always relied on a rickety old turntable pulled by a horse. This meant that an emergency produced frequent fiascos, with the horse in his field and reluctant to report for duty. So Mr Cramsie donated his own Bentley to the cause, and rushed to the fire station each time the alarm sounded.

The system worked well. Harry Penfold, whose job it had been to drive the horse, still sat on the turntable and directed operations when the fire was reached, but his seat was apparently a precarious one during the outward journey as Mr Cramsie eagerly squeezed every ounce of power out of his machine.

One of the most remarkable fireside sights was available one summer day in the mid 1920s, when Randal and Mrs Cramsie were returning from the Summer Cup meeting at Newbury. Randal was in full morning dress, his wife in an elegant coat with foxfur collar. They were almost home when the alarm bell rang and Randal put his foot down and drove straight on to the station, picking up the turntable and rushing on to the fire, still regally attired. It is not clear whether the Bentley protested, or perhaps Mrs Cramsie, but some time later the scheme was shelved and Mr Cramsie donated a brand-new fire engine to the service.

Randal Cramsie was successful, and his owners included various members of the country's gentry. One was Sir Daniel Cooper, whose son recently told Jim Cramsie a story against himself. Sir Daniel's son was at Cambridge University and admits to being a little dressy. He had a passion for horses, however, and knowing of his father's connections with Cramsie, asked if it might be possible for him to ride out at Lambourn one morning. His father agreed to fix it with Cramsie, and did so. Cooper, however, needed to rise at an unearthly hour to tackle the lengthy journey in whatever vehicle he possessed in those days. On time, he presented himself at the Cramsie residence, dressed in his usual riding clothes from home and feeling tired but excited at the morning's work ahead.

He was, apparently, a little taken aback that Randal himself answered the door, but after delivering his introductions, he concluded: 'I believe my father arranged that I might ride out for you this morning.' Randal Cramsie looked him up and down once more, then said: 'He did – but not dressed like that.' He then summarily closed the door, leaving one bewildered university student to spend several more hours driving back to Cambridge and pondering on the tradition of the time that jockeys should wear silks, clean breeches and sparkling boots even for morning work.

Another of Randal's owners was a man named Reggie Crawford. He had several horses in the yard, and occasionally used to dine with his trainer to discuss their form and prospects. On one such evening, it came to his mind that a particular favourite animal of his, recently injured, should now be back at work. 'Shall we see him gallop in the morning?' he asked. Cramsie, without so much as raising his eyes from his soup-bowl, answered, 'No.' Mr Crawford was not to be deterred and pressed for an explanation. 'Why is he not working yet? He must be fit.' The answer, still in a monotone, 'I shot him three weeks ago. He was useless.' Reggie Crawford spluttered furiously, finally simmering down enough to demand to know why his trainer had not at least had the decency to drop him a card revealing these facts. Randal at last put down his spoon, looked up and exploded: 'I have saved you three weeks' training fees. Do you mean to tell me you would like me to spend another penny-ha'penny on a stamp?'

I left Jim Cramsie as darkness fell and Lambourn froze. He drove back to his office to supervise the booking of boxes for more race meetings which would never take place.

The place looked much the same a fortnight later. Fresh falls of snow had occasionally topped up the misery in the interim, but the main handicap now came from frost, thick in the ground and showing no sign of budging. No racing had taken place in England since 7 December, and now the big Christmas programmes were under severe threat. Lambourn was not meant to withstand such an ice age. Life there was reduced from a gallop to an ugly shuffle, and the frowns of the racing folk deepened by the day. The village betting shop, generally a den of hot gossip and heavy wagers, eked out a miserable and often deserted existence via the greyhound cards and an occasional race-meeting in Ireland. But neither Harringay nor Limerick Junction could replace the real thing for the faithful of Lambourn.

In the pubs, even the optimists despaired and gave up talk of forthcoming races certain to join the list of phantoms. In Cripps', the village newsagent's, it is usually difficult to buy a copy of the *Sporting Life* after mid-morning; as the freeze bit deeper, a pile of the papers remained daily past lunchtime. Why study the form for non-existent races? Sheep huddled grimly together in the farms, and the Shrivenham Road became almost impassable to motorists as trainers with nowhere else to go sent out their string for endless days of exercise on the tarmac. Some days, half a mile in a car could take as long as fifteen minutes to complete, weaving gradually in and out of the horseflesh, directed by the lads riding at front and back of each string, vehicles often crossing on the wrong side of the road with a remarkably phlegmatic tolerance.

It was a bad time for the trainers. They were struggling to keep their horses tolerably fit, and when one of the worst blizzards in living memory hit the village on the afternoon of Sunday, 13 December, power was completely cut off and the routine processes of feeding and watering became a prolonged battle. Barry Hills, whose 112 horses had been confined to their boxes for three days, reported: 'It's desperate. I don't know how we are going to manage, but we'll just have to.'

Things were no better for the jockeys. Whereas the trainers were at least still being paid keep by their owners during the freeze, no racing meant no money for the majority of the country's jump jockeys.

Just a few were more fortunate. John Francome, certainly, divided his spare time quite profitably between the handyman jobs around his estate at which he had become so adept, and the hot batter of his chip shop where life went on much as before.

Another Lambourn jockey, less well endowed in terms of rides or winners when racing was in full flow, had also found his individual way of keeping the pounds trickling in. Martin O'Halloran a genial 29-year-old from Tipperary, had some time back realized that riding alone was never going to make his fortune, and enterprisingly augmented his earnings by qualifying in horse dentistry. It is not, I discovered, a profession in which he was likely to find much competition. In fact, it was as much as he could do to identify another wielder of the drill and pliers in England. Business had been encouragingly good in the five months since he graduated from an Oxford college following a two-year, part-time course which he had attended in free hours, morning, afternoon or evening, between riding engagements.

'I have done five hundred horses so far,' Martin told me in his quiet Irish burr as we sat in the cottage he lived in with wife Sandra, just before Christmas. Sandra is the daughter of flat trainer Doug Marks, and it was from him they had bought the property eleven months earlier. I gathered that Sandra had also been the prompt behind Martin's quest for knowledge about the inside of equine mouths.

'Whenever we used to go racing together, or just watch a string of horses at exercise, Sandra would point out one with his head in the air and wonder what was wrong inside his mouth. I decided it might be interesting to find out, and I was surprised to learn that it is virtually an untapped profession. Until I came along, most trainers had never thought much about their horses' teeth – but they can have toothache and decay just like the rest of us. Once I had finished the college course, I sent out cards to most of the trainers I know, asking if they would like me to look at their horses. The response has been very good, and I have done all those with Les Kennard, Nick Henderson, Nick Gaselee, David Elsworth and others.

'I don't use anaesthetic on the horses. A machine clamps their mouths open, and although I had my suspicions at first, they have almost all behaved them-selves while I've done the work. Only one, a great big hunter who had never really been handled at all, gave me real trouble, and eventually I had to give up on him. The work is mainly filing, and pulling out old and dead teeth. The more complicated jobs arise occasionally, such as putting a crown or a shell on a tooth. If things go well, I can get through forty patients a day. After that number, my arms get very tired and I would not be doing the job properly if I carried on. I started this because rides were pretty scarce, a couple of years ago. My retainer with Peter Cundell had finished, and I was finding it difficult to get restarted as a freelance. This gave me another string to my bow – and it's also something to do in the summer, when there is no racing.'

There was a touch of blarney in O'Halloran's very Irish eyes, but a lot of sense in the words he spoke, as befitted a man who had seen a good bit of life since leaving school in

Ireland at fourteen and coming to work for the man who is now his father-in-law. After spells with Marks and another flat trainer, Gavin Hunter, he quit racing temporarily to take a course in welding. Then he travelled to France, and later to America, before the wanderlust left him, the racing bug bit again and he came back to Berkshire to pick up his career.

O'Halloran now seemed at ease with his lot. The weather, he reported, had beaten him back the previous day when he set out for a dentistry job in Sussex, but he was not suffering too many hardships through the appalling conditions. 'I'm still playing squash five times a week,' he grinned. 'I'm pretty good at it now, you know.'

He filed another useless *Sporting Life* on a neat pile next to his front door, apologized for the padding with which he was attempting to keep out the draughts. Then he said, by way of a parting shot, 'Most jockeys are like me and could survive two or three months of a freeze-up like this without much suffering. Mind you, they will all plead poverty.'

Christmas in Lambourn falls into a set and social pattern. Racing traditionally recesses on 22 December, at which the village immediately celebrates in style at the annual Jockeys' Ball. The following days contain their generous share of house parties, stable parties and pub parties; on Christmas Day itself, those who can afford it tackle the traditional blow-out. I say this with reference to excess of weight rather than expense. Boxing Day features one of the biggest and best racing programmes of the winter season and jockeys putting up several pounds overweight with the excuse of an extra helping of turkey and roast are not viewed kindly by trainers who have probably spent a good part of Christmas Day working as normal.

This year, the village seemed more festive than usual in one sense, less so in another. The snow was reluctant to melt, lending an air of authenticity to the season, but the

Christmas card look was doing nothing for prospects of racing resuming, and rather less for the blood pressures of many of Lambourn's better-known residents. However, the morning of 23 December found Fulke Walwyn in surprisingly good humour. Saxon House was a warming haven against the mist and ice outside, and the grim-faced Michael Fish had just been on television predicting gloom and despondency, with further falls of snow, when I called on the old maestro. My mission was chiefly to gauge just how bad these conditions had been in comparison with previous years. Fulke, with his years of experience at Lambourn, was the oracle in such matters, and sure enough he provided an admirable answer.

'This is,' he said thoughtfully, 'the worst weather I have seen in several years, and in my memory it is quite unknown to suffer such conditions as early as December. Thinking back, the winters of 1947 and 1963 are the worst since I have been training, but even then I don't remember things getting bad before the turn of the year. It is a critical time of year for many people like myself. I have horses in the yard who have not yet run, and indeed have hardly been schooled in some cases. There is no possibility of getting any work into them at the moment, so the carefully-planned programmes for them are sabotaged. Disruptive weather never seems so bad in February, for instance, because by then all the horses would normally have run and many of them would find a rest more beneficial than damaging. But now, well . . .' Fulke pursed his lips and left the sentence unfinished.

I asked about his all-weather gallops. It was the wrong question to put. 'They are all useless now. All-weather except this weather, it seems. All we have done with the horses is walk them on the roads, and to do that we have had to get the staff salting down our drive, all of which takes time. It's a frustrating business and we can only pray that we'll wake up one morning soon and everything will be green again instead of white. At the moment, we all have to go through the motions of doing everything as usual, knowing damn well that there is no point to it all.'

The man with whom he had most sympathy, Walwyn went on, was downsman Eddie Fisher. 'Every day, he gives us all a report on conditions on the gallops,' he explained. 'Of course, we all know it is perfectly hopeless but Eddie is so conscientious. I think he would do virtually anything to get his gallops back in use again.'

At that moment a touch of Christmas cheer arrived in the form of a neighbour bearing gifts. Fulke smiled delightedly and broke off for a chat on the now mandatory topic of weather, before reseating himself and demanding some details of the Jockeys' Ball. He had not been present this year, adhering to his strict policy of early-to-bed, early-to-rise, but until recent years he had been an annual fixture at the function which brings together top jockeys, trainers, owners and hangers-on for a splendid blend of over-indulgence and lunacy which continues to an hour at which, on most other mornings of the year, Lambourn people are thinking about rising from their beds.

Staged in the country house environment of Elcot Park Hotel, ten miles from Lambourn, the event attracts racing folk from all over the south of England, many driving up from such outposts as Devon and East Kent. But, logistically, it is more attractive for the locals, and on most occasions it appears that half the population of Lambourn is in attendance. This year there were blower fires to keep the dining area tolerably warm, and a Caribbean steel band to induce the feeling of a more temperate climate. Cold turkey, hot mince pies and the customary scrum at the bars kept everyone's spirits bubbling, and there was the usual flood of money directed towards the Injured Jockeys' Fund and other worthwhile charities when the auction and raffle were held. Like almost everything else connected with the event, these were organized and supervised by two of Lambourn's most charming ladies. Miriam Francome needs virtually no introduction. The surname is enough to identify her as the stunning wife of champion jockey John. Dottie Channing-Williams is just as familiar a local face. She runs the Five Bells at Wickham, eight miles east of Lambourn and a pub much in use by jockeys, trainers and stable-lads, not to mention the many peripheral employees of the racing industry. Between them, they orchestrate the evening and generally succeed in raising several thousand pounds for the charities involved. It had reached an advanced hour by the time I turned in at my Hungerford hotel that night, and perhaps Mr Walwyn was not seeing me at my brightest the following morning. Maybe it was that which prompted his questions on the evening . . .

I was able to tell him that the cabaret, an annual feature of the function, had once more been performed by a motley crew of carollers who turned out to be the same half-dozen jockeys who had starred the year before and the year before that, namely John Francome, Oliver Sherwood, Steve Smith Eccles, Colin Brown, Malcolm Bastard and Steve Jobar. All except Smith Eccles live in or around Lambourn, and even he has strong connections. He arrived that night with Nick Henderson, and the rift which had seen their trainer-jockey partnership split before the season began had apparently been healed. Henderson was giving Smith Eccles rides again; Smith Eccles, who had caused a considerable stir by pulling out of a £10,000 retainer with the ambitious Alan Jarvis, was giving Henderson winners. The son of a Derbyshire miner who developed a passion for race-riding through his Dad's ten-bobs on the Saturday TV races, was once more at peace with the son of a city businessman who had gone his own way to find a niche in the equine world rather than the stockmarket. They made an odd couple, but it was good to see them together, and Steve was in his customarily boisterous mood as he belted out his part of the artistes' lightly-rehearsed version of 'We Three Kings'.

If they were honest, which they invariably are, the six would have admitted that this was not the greatest triumph of their cabaret career, dogged as they were by faulty microphones and an uncooperative hubbub from certain tables. But as ever they pooled their widely differing backgrounds in a good-humoured and enthusiastic attempt, which did ample justice to the spirit of the evening.

Francome, as usual, was turned to as peace-making ambassador, just as he is so frequently seen as spokesman for his profession. He came off the stage to be assailed by complaints from an elegantly dressed lady that she had been struck in the eye by a champagne cork.

At five o'clock on Christmas morning, Richard Head – parish councillor, trainer and army captain – had cause to leave the warmth of his bed in the splendid old house in Upper Lambourn he had bought from the Nugent family in 1968. He was sufficiently awake at this unwelcoming hour to be aware that outside it was still dark, cold and rather white. He was also aware of the type of noise not often associated with such a time of day, even in Lambourn. On peering out of an upstairs window to investigate, he perceived a man operating a rotivating machine on the sand track at the edge of the downs.

Even on Christmas morning, in the snow, the perfectionist Eddie Fisher was up and out early.

If Kempton Park and the annual King George VI Chase is the Christmas event which smacks of champagne and turkey to all racing followers, the same day's meeting at Newton Abbott is more evocative of brown ale and burned sausages. But, poor relation though it may be, the rustic Devon track lying in the mouth of the River Teign provided reason to celebrate on Boxing Day when it managed to stage the first race-meeting held in Britain for nineteen days.

The other seven Bank Holiday cards had been victims of the snow, ice and frost which gleefully alternated in their intensity. The Kempton programme, which was to have featured some of the finest horses from either side of the Irish Sea, was deemed hopeless several days before Christmas as London battled to extricate itself from the white plague. So the Lambourn contingent, large trainers and little punters alike, looked elsewhere for their Boxing Day sport, and found it down the M5 just short of the summer holiday haunt of Torbay.

So overwhelmed were the Newton Abbott executive by enthusiasm for their 'meeting on' verdict that they had to stretch the card from six to eight races to accommodate the wad of entries. They would also have had to find means of expanding their car park if the holiday lull had not allowed race-goers to freely abandon their cars on the streets outside the course.

Peter O'Sullevan, writing in the *Daily Express* shortly before Christmas and speculating on the possibility that Newton Abbott might be the sole surviving meeting, recalled a similar event many years ago, when the track bulged with a record crowd in excess of fifteen thousand. This time the attendance was not quite so large, but considering the remoteness of the course, the bitterness of the wind and the general downward trend in racing crowds, the fact that almost six thousand paid to watch was a quite staggering figure.

Leaving behind a Lambourn still trapped in the winter wilderness, I followed a thick line of snow down the motorway to Bristol. But there, at the point where the contingent from Berkshire and all points east turned sharply south for Newton Abbott, white turned to green as if a line was drawn across the country. In Somerset and Devon the only possible danger to sporting events seemed to come from flooding, and although clouds scudded keenly across the sky, the sun was even shining welcomingly as I descended the hill from Kingsteignton towards the course.

At intervals along the route, I had spotted the tell-tale signs of other cars heading for racing – a pair of binoculars on the back shelf, a couple of trilby-clad heads, or a *Sporting Life* being keenly scanned. And now I could see a great deal more, a queue in fact, stretching back several hundred yards from the entrance to the track, past the site for a new supermarket, a couple of anonymous factory sheds and a row of rusted petrol pumps. Not very prepossessing, maybe, but at least there was the promise of action.

The track itself is squeezed uncomfortably between the road, the river and some railway sidings. All forms of human transport meet here, you might say. Today, as it admitted a hundred more Devonian accents every few minutes, it was also the meeting place for many racing folk who had been starved of each other's company for almost three weeks.

The Lambourn representation lost a little of its class when Fulke Walwyn decided to withdraw Glen Berg from the Handicap Chase, but Fred Winter sent two runners to a course at which he does not even appear in the leading trainers list, so seldom does he normally have the need to patronize it. Nick Gaselee was present to see his Leading Artist run, and of the village's jockeys, Colin Brown, Ben de Haan and John Francome had all made the trip to shiver in the corrugated-iron weighing-room.

Familiar faces could be seen among the crowd, too. 'Dodger', real name Simon McCartney, had driven down from Wales to continue his devoted one-man fight to beat the bookies. 'Dodger' makes a living out of gambling, and specializes in National Hunt racing. The story goes that he often tells the jockeys when they are going to win, rather than vice-versa.

Up in the buffet room, nine women scuttled about feverishly behind the counter, attempting to cope with the type of rush Newton Abbott sees all too rarely. Among the new coats, fat cigars and chatter about presents, bowls of tomato soup were drunk, and many dozens of mince pies eaten. They were out of a packet, but exceedingly good cakes.

Out on the course, John Francome rode a winner for Sheik Ali Abu Khamsin, and then departed for his windswept, hilltop home, leaving the crowd to scratch their heads over some difficult punting and the stewards, whose job on such bitter days is unenviable, to shiver on their exposed, open-air rostrum.

Marilyn Scudamore, wife of Francome's closest title challenger, presented the women's side of racing's return. 'I was so relieved it was on,' she said. 'Peter has been getting steadily more miserable every day that racing has been abandoned.' His misery was not completely lifted, however, as six rides failed to bring him a single winner and he slipped further behind the riding prince of Lambourn.

It was not, overall, a triumphant Lambourn day. Both the Winter entries were soundly beaten and Gaselee's Leading Artist fell, out in the country. Nick, impassively philosophical, swapped some consoling comments with his owners and then they all trooped up the wooden staircase into a door marked 'Directors' Bar'. Sometimes it can be a comfort to have the right connections.

5·Businesses and Pleasures

MOST people in Lambourn will claim, justifiably, that their hours are long even if their work is enjoyable, but there are few who literally open all hours for business. One such establishment, however, is the Ridgway Veterinary Practice, tucked in between the village square and a batch of new houses and arguably the most vital of all the ancilliary professions to the racing industry.

For many years, this has been the largest practice in the Lambourn area, and virtually all the trainers in the vicinity have come to rely upon the skills of its seven vets, four of whom are partners in the business. Of these, the longest-serving, and thus probably the senior partner, is a mild, kindly Irishman who looks, at first glance, as if he could imitate Harry Worth without trying too hard. The facial resemblance is not entirely misleading, as Frank Mahon's sense of humour is well known and well employed. He is among the most compelling raconteurs I found in Lambourn and provides the most convivial of company. He is also, by all accounts, an outstandingly good vet.

One of five brothers, Frank came to England twenty-eight years ago after failing to find the right opening for his qualifications at The Curragh. Newmarket, he discovered, was similarly overburdened with willing vets, so he settled on Lambourn, and helped build up the Ridgway practice into the impressive concern it is today.

'There will always be employment for good vets in this area,' he says. 'Our problem has simply been in financing the technical improvements which we feel are necessary to give a proper service.' Lambourn, in this regard, is overlooked by the Horseracing Levy Board, who have supported veterinary research in the predominantly flat-racing centre of Newmarket but gave no assistance to the Ridgway practice in its expansion. Their premises now comprise offices, laboratories – stocked with eye-opening equipment far too complex for this layman to explain – consulting rooms and a stable block containing eighteen boxes. 'They are full most of the time, with horses recovering from treatment or being detained for observation,' explained Frank as we looked round. The inmates, when I visited, included Monkey Corners and Bealnablath, two luckless animals from Nicky Henderson's yard, Stan Mellor's highly-rated novice hurdler Baz Bombati and a plain-looking Arab mare who had been badly and messily hurt in foaling. All types are treated the same here.

Set apart from the main administrative block of the practice is Frank's pride and joy, the operating theatre. He designed it himself and because of its innovative features there were a number of false starts and teething troubles, the last of which had not been resolved. It cost £20,000 to construct, which may sound expensive but remains a pittance when set against the overall cost of £250,000 to equip the practice or, more significant, the obvious need for it.

'There are some days when the theatre is in constant use,' said Frank. 'A queue even forms, and those waiting who might be urgent cases for surgery might have to use the hay of the barn outside as an emergency operating table.

'We are on call twenty-four hours a day and every day of the year for emergency cases, and there have been weeks when we have done three or four operations during the night – chiefly when there is an outbreak of cholic. On other occasions, we might go for three days or so without having to use the theatre at all.'

The theatre has two entrances, one from the barn and one from a control room – a converted kitchen, really, with various switches and levers which Frank detailed for me, and storage space for the essentials of surgery. Inside the theatre, my first impression was of a prison cell for dangerous criminals. The walls are green and thickly padded and the floor is made of sprung rubber with a special pour-on surface to prevent skidding. Cracks had developed in the floor during the bitterly cold weather, and the surface was about to be replaced, but the principle had been proved sound.

'All the padding is essential, simply to prevent horses hurting themselves when they come into the room in a drugged and probably frightened state,' said Frank. 'They can bounce off these walls as often as they like, and it is very unlikely they will come to any harm.'

Horses are brought in from the barn, having been given an anaesthetic. They are then left in the theatre alone until they pass out, whereupon the clever part of the routine comes into play. Hobs, bought and imported from Kentucky by Frank Mahon, are attached to the drugged horse's legs, and a motorized winch drags him automatically into the centre of the floor. At the touch of a lever, the slab on which the horse is now lying is lifted by a motorized scissors action and becomes a most effective, adjustable operating table. When the surgery is complete, the animal is once more lowered to floor level and left to recover in his own time.

'We use three people on most operations,' explained Frank. 'A surgeon, an anaesthetist at the "sharp end" of the patient, and a girl to do the preparations, the clipping and the cleaning. But if, during the night, there is a simple but urgent operation and we are pushed for staff, it has been known for the whole process to be conducted single-handed. It isn't very difficult once you know the routine. There is a good bit of heartbreak in our job, but mainly it belongs to other people,' he added. 'I get a great kick, even now, out of getting injured horses right and seeing them go back to the racetrack and win. That is my job satisfaction.'

Frank's thoughtful, bespectacled face and measured tread are well known in the Five Bells, his favourite pub, where he sips wine – the drink to which he confines himself these days – and swaps anecdotes with the locals in their flat caps and old tweed jackets. 'Reminiscing is a warming pastime,' he says before launching into another memory from long-ago Ireland or more recent Lambourn.

His interest in racing, which is still considerable, centres on National Hunt and is far more concerned, oddly enough, with the jockeys than the horses. 'Horses are my business and I follow their progress, particularly those trained locally,' he says. 'But it is the jockeys who fascinate me. For years, jump jockeys have been my idols and although I may not be the greatest student of raceform, I do make a study of riding styles.'

Frank Mahon's heroes began with Bryan Marshall, champion jockey in 1948 and, according to the senior vet, one of the all-time stylists. 'I got to know Bryan well, and liked him enormously. But his great trouble was his long-windedness. I once travelled with him from Lambourn to Dublin, driving to Heathrow and flying over. I was interested to ask him about the previous year's Grand National, and posed the question as we set off out of the village up Hungerford Hill. Bryan's answer began several months before the race itself and took so many diversions that we had touched down in Ireland before he had crossed the second fence at Aintree!'

Frank recalls Dave Dick – 'an Errol Flynn type jockey, larger than life'; Bobby Beasley – 'brilliant but erratic'; and Fred Winter. 'Now Fred might not have had the style of others, but he had an extraordinary capacity to work throughout a race and drive out a horse, willing it to win for him . . .' Frank's opinions on jockeys are crisp and firm, and there are at least two former champions, now highly regarded in different fields, to whom he credits precious little talent. He talks lucidly, too, of Lambourn's training fraternity and calls Fulke Walwyn 'the greatest of them all . . . how can a man of seventy-one summon the motivation to keep sending out big winners? That really is greatness.'

It was time for Frank to go home to the house in Eastbury where he and his wife live. He had the enjoyable feeling of not knowing what the next morning would bring. 'Only last week, I was called out on a round trip of nearly four hundred miles to treat a horse in the north, and although most of my work is local, I am not in the least restricted. Each year, for instance, I go to Kentucky and Kenya on working trips, picking up a lot of useful knowledge and, sometimes, equipment.'

Despite all his connections, however, he very seldom appears at race meetings. 'When I lived in Ireland, I flew over for eleven successive Cheltenham Festivals and thought I would be there forever. But I never go now, simply because it is too close. At Cheltenham, Newbury, or any other course in this area, I can hardly get through the gate before some trainer, who might be a good friend and a very nice bloke, collars me and leads me off to look at a horse with a swelling in his leg. Immediately, my day's pleasure ceases and I am back at work. So nowadays, I prefer to watch on television, and only go racing when I am away from home.'

Frank Mahon, in truth, is rarely away from work. 'The partners in the practice are on call unless they say they are off,' he explains. 'The employed staff take half-days off, but they all get upset if they miss anything. Our lasting nightmare is the horses who go through barbed wire – they really are messy jobs. But even then, there is the theatre close at hand now, and I believe it is a comfort to trainers, as well as to us. One of the priorities of our profession is to provide a consolation to trainers that when things go wrong, we have the ability and the equipment to put them right.'

There was no red carpet welcome for me at the old forge on Hungerford Hill. Lunchtime, I had been advised, was the time to be sure of catching Tony Halestone at home, and catch him I had done. It appeared, however, that he was not overjoyed at the prospect of the interview.

Mr Halestone is the village blacksmith. Or one of them, at least. He plies his trade from an old timber structure which looks, inside, just the epitome of the forges one sees in pictures. Horseshoes were scattered in their dozens around the potholed stone floor, while ancient, low beams and rusted lights gazed down on the two furnaces, only one of which was alight. A map of the country hung on one wall, a couple of saucy calendars on another, while a gleaming new steel ladder looked out of place amid the necessary antiquity.

Just across the yard is Mr Halestone's house. The phone was ringing as I approached the front door, and it was to ring three times more in the next fifteen minutes. It might have been lunchtime, but there was no let-up for a blacksmith in Lambourn.

At first viewing, Tony Halestone was gruff, impatient and showed a fair impression of antagonism. He faced half away from me as he ate his toasted lunch at the kitchen table, and answered my questions in monosyllables and mock irony. One of his assistants, seated across the table, made a joke and was rebuked with a jerk of Mr Halestone's head in my direction and a sharp: 'It's bad enough having him here, without you starting.'

Thankfully, it soon became apparent that beneath the veneer was a sense of humour and, I dare say, a warm personality . . . I was not with him long enough to go further. Casting anxious glances at the clock on top of the cooker, he pointed out that a long afternoon of work awaited him, with calls to be made right up past eight in the evening. 'I work ten to twelve hours almost every day,' he explained. 'Some Sundays too, especially at the busiest times of year when jump racing overlaps with the flat. Today is a typical day – I was out of the house before eight, and apart from this quick lunch I shan't be back much before nine tonight. The phone starts ringing at about seven most mornings, and if I'm lucky it stops about ten at night. I get plenty of emergency calls, but not in the middle of the night, I'm pleased to say. But I don't know why you're talking to me anyway. I'm not a local.'

Which, when I was fully abreast of his background, seemed particularly modest, as the Halestone family first came to Lambourn forty-four years ago when Tony, who was born in Staffordshire, was of junior school age.

'I never rode horses as a boy,' he recalled, loosening up a trifle. 'Nor did I have any interest in racing. But once you come to Lambourn and get involved in this business, it's pretty near impossible to ignore it.'

The business was started by Tony's father. 'He was a gypsy, I'm told,' he said surprisingly. 'But he taught me the trade, alright. I was apprenticed to him in 1949 and went into the business in my own right in 1954,' added Tony, settling on the latter date only after some mental calculations, interrupted by yet another phone call.

Tony Halestone is a large man, with greying hair, dark eyes and a very expressive face. Altogether, not a figure I would care to find among the opposition if I was a front-row rugby forward. His voice, once it lost its initial sharp edge, was gentle enough, and his face crinkled into the odd smile as he related his reasons for going into a trade many people outside the intimate horse world believe to be dying.

'I didn't have the brains to do anything else, it's as simple as that. I suppose it was the natural thing to follow my father. But you don't need a brilliant mind to do this job – just to be fit, tough and have a capacity for work.'

The Halestone company, which comprised the boss, two qualified men and one lad just completing the stringent four-year apprenticeship which includes a year at college and both written and practical examinations, share most of the Lambourn pickings, in business terms, with another old family concern, the Aldertons. Roy Alderton, who lives in the village, inherited the job from his father Vic, born at the turn of the century and now living in the neighbouring hamlet of Eastbury. Tony Halestone smiled again when he mentioned Vic, for whom he plainly felt affection despite the business rivalry.

'We do seven of the major racing yards, which accounts for about 250 to 280 horses. The rest of our work is chiefly on the studs of the area, as far out as Slough and Aylesbury. Racing trainers don't like blacksmiths, you know. They see us as a necessary evil and complain all the time about the expense,' he revealed. 'It costs them £11 to get a horse shod by me . . . it'll be £12 soon when my prices go up . . . and the frequency depends on where they send them. A set of shoes can last anything from six days to six weeks. The average is about three weeks, but it will be a lot less if the horses spend much time trotting on the roads. Then they should expect the shoes to go very quickly.

'I never go racing. I'm still not very interested. I certainly don't follow form, and the only real satisfaction I get from one of the horses I have done is when I get a couple of quid tip if it wins.'

He finished his first cup of tea and started on his second. I turned to the subject of injuries, because I imagined his to be a rather hazardous profession, working so close to such large feet shod in such painful metal. He did not deny it. 'You are bound to get the odd kick, but you soon learn where to stand, and how to avoid them. But I'll tell you what – anyone who has been in this job for twenty years or more will end up either with a hernia or bad back trouble. I should know . . . I've had both.'

One man in Lambourn has worked for the Queen, the

Queen Mother, Prince Charles and the Sultan of Oman. He has also worked for the majority of the trainers, jockeys and stable-lads in the vicinity, and about 85 per cent of the area's racehorses carry his wares on their back.

Cyril Bentick is the village's resident saddler. The only saddler, in fact, although there are others who travel the area in vans, visiting the yards personally and, according to Cyril's grim description, 'selling them things that we could do so easily'.

Headquarters for Cyril and his workforce of eight is a white stone building just past the car park of The George on the road to Eastbury, the village side of those other haunts of racing lads, the chip shop and the laundrette. 'E. J. Wicks – Racing and Hunting Saddlers' is printed in large and quite distinguished lettering on the side, and there is a crest underneath. The shop front is less impressive. The windows wear the dust and grime of many months without a clean and many splashes from trucks on the road which passes perilously close. Even dirtier is the graffiti which has been daubed in the dust by mischievous fingertips. A square black sign announces suitably solemnly that a solicitor is present after lunch every Friday; it does not say whether he specializes in gambling bankrupts.

The shop itself is wide but shallow and smells sweetly of leather. Saddles, rugs, reins, boots and every conceivable racing accessory give the place a look of joyful jumble, an image perpetuated when one picks a path behind the counter and into the hives of industry beyond. Staff work in several small rooms, and I found Cyril in the farthest hive of all, surrounded by part-completed products, a smiling middle-aged lady working on a machine and a radio from which Ed Stewart was disgorging another batch of family favourites.

Mr Bentick has strikingly red hair. It was once even redder, I understand, and explains the otherwise morbid impression one might gain from his long-standing nickname, Blood. He has a lined face and a ready, friendly smile, and although he has lived in Lambourn more than forty years, enough of his Lancashire background is still apparent in his accent to evoke vague analogies with a Coronation Street character.

In many respects, Cyril has certainly seen life, racing life in particular. He left Great Crosby in 1939 and came to Lambourn as an apprentice jockey on the flat. His memories of those years are vivid. 'We did have some times, you know. Nobody now can appreciate how bad the conditions were that we had to live in. They were unsanitary, filthy and I shudder today to even think about it. But we still managed to laugh our way through and enjoy ourselves.'

For some years, Cyril worked part-time for the saddlers on his free afternoons. Jim Wicks owned and ran the business in those days, although it had been founded by his brother-in-law at the turn of the century. Jim's daughter Sylvia was the company secretary but, surprisingly, she did not meet Cyril until a local dance brought them together. For the past thirty years they have been married.

On many of the afternoons when Cyril clocked in as a helper, an interested spectator crept into the shop to watch the saddlery art in action. He was only a lad then, but already hooked on racing, and soon to move from the downland of Lambourn to the heathland of Newmarket. His name was Lester Piggott. 'He was there most days,' Cyril relates, 'always eager to watch Mr Wicks at work. It's funny isn't it, that we supply him with some of his equipment now – and feel proud to do so.' Perhaps not quite so proud, though, as when they were asked to produce a racing rug for Prince Charles when he set off on his brief but highly publicized venture as an owner and rider of National Hunt horses. 'One of Nick Gaselee's lads came in with the order. He wanted the three feathers on his rug, and I thought it might turn out a bit difficult. But, by chance, I came across a girl in Didcot who does this type of specialist embroidery. Between us, we were able to provide exactly what he wanted. That one gave me a lot of satisfaction,' added Cyril.

His regular turnover for the royal family earned Cyril and Sylvia an invitation to a recent garden party at Buckingham Palace. And, among his 1982 orders currently receiving the attention of the workforce was one worth £9,000 for the Sultan of Oman.

Not all business is quite so upmarket, however. The saddlers get by, day to day, on the patronage of Lambourn's trainers and lads, plus a few who choose to buy there from outside the area. There were certainly no outward signs of the recession here; everyone appeared to be flat out and Cyril confirmed that this was the case. 'I have been working seven days a week, eight in the morning until 5.30 at night, plus a few nights. It is very hard to keep up with demand,' he explained, although anxiously dispelling any impression that he was complaining. 'Everything we do is handsewn apart from clothing and the rubber grips for reins. But I must say we buy in most of the saddles now. It makes much more sense, because it takes three days, beginning to end, to produce a handmade one.'

Cyril bought a one-third share in the business in 1965 and only two years ago his son, Malcolm, joined him and they took it over completely. Everyone in Lambourn knows Cyril now – and he knows almost everybody although like many others he points out the difference in the place since the new estates sprang up. 'Up to a few years ago I really did know everyone by name,' he says. 'But the motorway changed all that. It's still a unique village though, don't you think? I have relations in the north and when they come here to visit they don't understand the place. They think everyone in Lambourn must be Chinese, I think.'

Not only was Cyril a jockey – and one who was still light

enough at less than eight stone to ride in the 1959 Derby – but, later, a permit-holder whose horses were generally ridden by his daughter Sandra, now secretary to Nicky Henderson at Windsor House. 'I never did better than a second place,' confesses Cyril sadly. 'And eventually I packed it up due to lack of time. It was disappointing for Sandra.'

So now Cyril Bentick is just the village saddler. Well, not really. He is also one of those chaps whose personality invites conversation and I have no doubt there is little goes on in Lambourn that Cyril doesn't know. 'I suppose I do have my finger on the pulse of the village here,' he says. 'I know I'm always swamped by tips. But I ignore most of them . . .'

Out of habit, I attracted the attention of barmaid Flo on the stroke of 10.30 and ordered my final drink of the evening. The back bar of The Red Lion – the cocktail bar, to give it its formal title – had been pleasantly relaxed, with maybe a dozen in the company, the conversation wide-ranging and the hectic hubbub of the Thursday night disco in the cavernous public bar suitably remote.

I was down to the last few sips and preparing to go to bed. I was staying at the pub that night, and my room was perfectly adequate even if the floorboards did creak and the radiators stayed chillingly cold until long after dark. It was not the type of hotel to which the RAC would be handing out stars, but I was tired and the bed was still welcoming.

So preoccupied had I been with these thoughts that I had failed to notice the lack of the customary calls of 'last orders' and 'time'. I was soon to find out why, as what seemed like hundreds of people began filing through the door and squeezing up to the bar. Most of them were in their late teens or early twenties, some trendily dressed and perspiring from the exertions of the dance floor. I expected the manager to eject them; instead, Flo – now wearing her well-trained 'don't panic' expression behind the tiny bar, worked her way conscientiously through the auction-ring of potential buyers. It was clear, at least, that the bar was not closed; music soon began to pipe through speakers and, on seeking explanation, I was informed that drinks were served until two in the morning. The Red Lion had a music licence to meet the needs of late drinkers, and there was no shortage of takers.

My early night never transpired. I did not notice the floorboards creaking, and if the radiator had remained off all night I am not certain it would have concerned me.

Reconstructing events through heavy eyes at breakfast – I was gratified to note the discreet lighting and the *sotto voce* style of the waiter – it struck me as slightly surprising that a place like Lambourn should have such a regular late-night watering-hole, but reassuring that it should be based in an old room surrounded by racing prints and featuring low beams and a genuine well, preserved and popularly sat on, next to the bar. Supervising these nocturnal revelries was a cheery Scotsman, with whom I had exchanged a few words the previous night as he sat at the bar with Marje from the newsagent's, just prior to the invasion of disco-goers. I sought him out after breakfast and, as we picked our way over the prostrate body of the pub's Alsatian to a seat in the window, I wondered aloud at his resilience in the face of so many late nights.

Jimmy Gould raised the eyebrows on his full, rounded face, and nodded. 'Late in the week, when we really get full, I am up until four in the morning. It's always that, by the time we have got everybody out and cleared up. Then I'm out of bed again at 7.45 to sort things out for the new day.'

A stocky man with close-cropped hair, Jimmy took over as manager of The Red Lion in 1980. He had been coming to the pub, with varying degrees of regularity, for thirty years. For some years, indeed, he had lived next door, in

The George, and it had been his hope to take on that pub. But, not being a married man, his offer was declined.

Before his return to Lambourn, Jimmy had worked as odd-job man for a multi-millionaire, based chiefly in India and Sri Lanka. And before that, he had played football. No mean player, either. The soccer reference books confirm that J. Gould appeared twice for Scotland before his career was ended by an incident he prefers to push to the back of his mind these days. Suffice to say it made headlines at the time, and Jimmy has not been involved in the game since.

He was pleased to be back in Lambourn. His friends had always been in the area, he said, and he had long been a devotee of racing – National Hunt mainly, but he had no objection to the flat. Both provided tips, after all, and as Jimmy said, 'I can't believe anyone is in a position to get more tips than me. It's why I'm always skint.' He went on, 'My memories of this place go back to the early 1950s. It was always a drinking pub then, not somewhere to eat or to stay as it is now. I used to come in with Sammy Wragg and Jimmy Lindley and play darts in that front bar. I think it has changed a lot, both this pub and the village itself. But then I am looking at it through older eyes now.'

We were interrupted by the arrival of a man with a furtive face and an ill-disguised wig. He was a loud and unlovable spiv, known by sight if not character to most people in Lambourn, and potentially amusing company for five minutes if he did not take himself so seriously.

'He claims that only royalty is good enough for him,' confided Jimmy when he had gone. 'He bets every day of his life, on dogs if not horses. He talks in thousands of pounds, yet carries a plastic bag instead of a suitcase.' Clearly, he was not sorry to see him leave the pub.

It was now approaching eleven, and already the place was showing increasing signs of activity. Two salesmen asked Jimmy for directions to one of the yards in the village; Jimmy gave them precisely, unhesitatingly. 'You soon get to know where everybody lives,' he said. 'You see, about 80 per cent of the people who come in this pub are stable-lads. It's a big proportion, and they are spread around many yards. So I soon come to identify with them and their horses.'

I asked if there was ever any trouble in The Red Lion. He shrugged. 'I came here soon after the introduction of the two o'clock licence, and that has obviously made a difference. But the local lads are not trouble-makers. When we do get any, it is normally caused by drunks arriving from outside the village. They come here from Newbury, Wantage, even Swindon, you know. Racing lads in Lambourn know what they want. It is the three Bs – birds, booze and betting – only they aren't sure in which order they like them. There are plenty who come in here day after day and get rid of 90 per cent of their wages at the bar. It's frightening, really, but they seem happy enough, and certainly keep the place going.

'We have thirteen letting rooms here now, and they are not always full. Occasionally, there are things going on in the village which help. Recently the BBC were making a film here, and they took all the rooms for weeks on end.'

Lunchtime was approaching and Jimmy had to make his apologies and hurry to change some beer barrels. The lads would be in soon. He marched off down the corridor which separates front from back bar, generation from generation. The reception area is seedy, the toilets are not short of graffiti and most of the place needs a lick of paint. But this is a lads' pub, where hair is let down rapidly and regularly. Those who want a quiet drink and a chat, or a discreet evening with a new girlfriend, use other pubs. But The Red Lion has its place in Lambourn, and thrives on it.

When Peter and Maureen Jackson arrived to take over The George, it looked like a scene from *The Sweeney* after a particularly violent pub brawl. The floor was covered in dust, ashes and meal tickets and the furniture, such as it was, resembled something from another age. At that awful moment, they were all for giving up the idea and going home to Yorkshire.

With good cheer and fortitude, however, they turned the large single bar into a cross between a very good pub and a living-room. The cosy side of the bar, farthest from the dart board, is where Harry Foster, Lambourn's oldest lad, sits with his Guinness each morning and evening, and where another half-dozen lugubrious old boys park themselves for a daily session of reminiscing. It is looked over by a colour television, unusual in any bar, and constantly clucked over by the beaming Maureen, who serves meals, pulls pints, listens to everyone's problems and manages to smile phlegmatically through her own. Almost the perfect landlady.

The George is a social step up from The Red Lion. Stable-lads come here, too, but they are generally more smartly dressed and sober. They know there will be no rock music and no late licence; The George shuts on time each night.

Parish councillors come here, like chairman Ted Brind. Trainers pop in for a half-pint before lunch. Businessmen and tourists use it as a stop-over in their travels, and in that it is a very good find as the rooms are airy, comfortable and cheap. Like most pubs, not to mention houses, in the district, racing prints abound. But a couple take pride of place. They are of Bali George, the horse owned by Peter and Maureen and raced over hurdles. He was there pride and joy, and seldom did an evening in The George pass without some reference to his potential or future races. But one day, just before Cheltenham, everything changed, and for a few minutes they stopped being efficient at the business of running a pub and became dejected racehorse owners, feeling the frustrations known to so many in the village. Bali George had a serious tendon injury, and would not race again for at least two years. Perhaps never. Even Maureen's smile slipped a little, that day.

The Maltshovel, sited near the gates of Fulke Walwyn's yard, is the local for every lad working in Upper Lambourn. The Wheelwright's Arms, opposite the betting shop, is the daily haunt of many long-standing residents of Lambourn village. Both are small, serve good beer and treat unfamiliar faces with initial suspicion, simply because they seldom see any.

Lunchtime in the Wheelwright's is pretty quiet and unhurried. In the small back bar, a few elderly folk discuss family problems before slipping quickly on to the subject of the afternoon's jump racing. Across the hatchway, in the larger public bar, a group of muffled figures have pints and dominoes laid on the table in front of them. They talk little, just continue with the serious business of playing.

'The Malt', as it is colloquially known, is altogether livelier. The pool table in one of the two tiny bars is occupied, as it always seems to be, while in the main bar a furiously funny round of spoof is being conducted by half a dozen lads from the Walwyn yard. They are here every lunchtime, mixing with a few residents of the hamlet. It is part of their private world, a world which an outsider cannot easily understand.

6·Lambourn Lads

ONLY in the language peculiar to racing could Harry Foster be called a lad at the age of sixty-four. A miniature, elfin-like figure, whose permanent attire includes flat cap and breeches, Harry is an institution in Lambourn. Not one to hide his light under any bushel or barstool, he even insists himself that 'there will never be another stable-lad like me'. He is probably right.

Harry was born in the Yorkshire colliery town of Pontefract, which has a quaint flat-racing track and not much else. Even as a boy, he was unusually small, but by the age of eleven he had had his first bout as an amateur boxer, in the neighbouring town of Dewsbury. He scaled less than six stone, but still won, and went on winning.

Later in life, when serving in the Heavy Artillery for three war years, he was unbeaten flyweight champion of the Army. Boxing has remained his second sporting love, worth relating if only for its incongruity. Harry Foster looks every inch a stable-lad, but his distinct lack of those inches – in height, reach and girth – would seem to stamp him a non-starter with gloves. Just once, in his long and eventful racing life, has the fighter in him come to the surface. It resulted in a scrap with a workmate in a Lambourn yard, and Harry moved on to pastures new. He has done that more than a few times in his fifty working years, but the last sixteen of them have been spent happily settled at Uplands, home for Fred Winter's formidable team of horses.

Harry lives in a small house of his own, opposite the church in the very centre of the village. He has been parted from his wife for some years; his two sons have long since grown up and gone their separate ways; so Harry lives alone, cooking and coping for himself. But, he will tell you defiantly, it is the way he likes to be. This remarkable little character with the sharp, lived-in face and the short, scuttling legs, has been an independent type ever since he left home at fourteen to find work with horses in Epsom. He had known for years it was what he wanted to do. 'Instead of doing my schoolwork, I had always studied racing. I used to bet on horses while I was at school, you know – not much, just tanners and shillings because there wasn't a lot of cash about in them days.'

Harry did not find the end of his rainbow in Epsom, so he hurried onwards. He knew that Newmarket was the country's biggest racing centre and reasoned there must be work there for the likes of him. He was right. 'My first job in a Newmarket yard earned me sixpence a week spending money, plus a quarterly allowance for clothes,' he relates. 'But I didn't care, so long as I had enough to get by on, with a bit left over for a bet.'

At first, the ambition nurtured by most lads to graduate to jockey status was rife within Harry. But he found rides hard to come by. 'Lads could not claim the weight allowance in those days, and not many trainers wanted to put you up.' He did, however, ride eighteen winners during his long racing career, the last of them for Major Nelson's Lambourn stable at the ripe old age of forty-nine. All of the winners were on the flat, but Harry has good reason to remember his one and only ride under National Hunt rules. 'It was in a hurdle race at Cheltenham, and I fell early on,' he says ruefully.

Harry Foster was twenty-two when he came to Lambourn. The gypsy in his soul had urged a move from Newmarket, and Lambourn was the natural next stop. In the years following the end of the war, he worked for Frank Templeman, Ossie Bell and then Fulke Walwyn. His memories of those times are as fresh as if it had been yesterday. 'Lambourn was swarming with punters from London. They drove down in their cars, and the pubs were packed every night. Everybody wanted information and blokes like me had a marvellous time. I could earn the equivalent of a week's wages for one tip. They were good days, but they didn't last because the newspapers started giving their own tipping services. There was no longer any call for the local knowledge.'

If Harry looks back with a touch of nostalgic regret to the days gone by, he will tell you sharply he is perfectly content with his modern life. It is predictable, unambitious and would not suit everyone. But Lambourn's oldest lad is not complaining. His life revolves around four places – his home, the yard, the pub and the betting shop. One way and another, he manages to rotate the demands of each to everyone's satisfaction.

Each day begins with an alarm call at six o'clock. 'I wouldn't wake without the alarm. Most nights I'm out in the pub past midnight, and I would sleep for twelve hours afterwards if I could.' He makes himself a cup of tea, then walks the half-mile to Uplands. 'Sometimes I'm late,' he admits. 'And there have been times when I've been too drunk to get to work . . . but that hasn't happened very often really.'

After feeding and mucking out, he rides out first lot at 7.45. His two horses this season were Al Kuwait, a tidy performer on the flat just progressing to hurdles, and Jarvis Bay, who had nicked his first race of the campaign on an optimistic objection which was upheld to the surprise of jockey John Francome and the relief of Harry's finances.

Breakfast is eaten in the lads' hostel, behind the yard, at 9.30. Many of the younger boys tuck into bacon and eggs, with piles of bread and butter. Harry contents himself with tea and toast, although it has not always been that way. Years ago, most of the lads brought sandwiches with them. Harry apparently felt he was being badly done by his wife and forever complained that, while others had interesting fillings in their sandwiches, his were always filled with rubbish. The story goes that his wife finally tired of such moaning, coming from a man who was evidently a trifle forgetful when it came to passing on the money to pay bills. The next day Harry opened up his sandwich box and found two slices of bread with a particularly interesting filling – a rent book.

After the second lot of horses has been ridden out, the feeding completed and the yard tidied, Harry retires for lunch. He has one pint of Guinness in The George, another in The Red Lion next door, then bustles across the road to his house where he cooks himself a meal then catches up on some sleep in front of the fire. By four o'clock, he is back at Uplands, busying himself diligently 'because I can't cope with being still at work'.

'I have a lot of nervous energy; I like getting on with my work, getting it done and then sweeping up the yard, or helping the head lad. I'm a person who must keep on the move – the only time I stand around is when I've got a drink in my hand at night.'

The racing results will filter up to the yard and Harry will know whether his traditional lunchtime walk to the village branch of Ladbrokes was worthwhile exercise. Evening stables are at 5.30, and half an hour later Harry is on his way home again. He eats a light dinner then sets off back to The George. 'I'm always in there by nine of a night. I'll have a couple in there, then move on to The Red Lion. I'll drink anything really – beer, Scotch or brandy, and I don't mind having a laugh and a joke with some of my friends. But I don't talk silly and I don't act silly. I never have done,' he says with a hint of reproach.

Like most lads, Harry does twelve days on, then has a weekend off. He will spend his free Saturday in the pub and the betting shop and reckons to make money. 'I might have a score or two on a race,' he says. 'Of course you get all kinds of tips up here. But you learn what to take in and what to ignore.'

Harry Foster was responsible for Lanzarote, who pro-vided Fred Winter with his third Champion Hurdle triumph as a trainer. Harry rates him the best horse he has 'done' – 'because he won me a good few races'. Perhaps surprisingly, his second choice is Sonny Somers, that marvellous old chaser who was still racing and winning when long past the human age of consent.

It is impossible to spend much time in Lambourn without recognizing the familiar sight of Harry's urgent march around the village. If you do not actually know where he is going, you can have a pretty fair idea judging by the time of day.

He goes home to Yorkshire most summers, and his guv'nor never pesters him about coming back on time. Recently, he branched out and had a summer holiday across the Atlantic, in South Carolina. In the bar of The George, his Guinness in front of him, his cap wedged on his head, the stories at the end of his tongue, I wondered just what the Americans made of Harry Foster.

It was a safe bet, so I heard, that I would find the man known to all as Crottie, sitting on a bar stool in The Maltshovel. I did. He is there every day, he admitted, either at lunchtime or in the evening or, very often, both. At least, I think that is what he said. Paddy Crottie is the type who seems to build on an already broad Irish accent to make his sentences virtually unintelligible to bland Anglo-Saxons like myself. Notwithstanding that, he is an intriguing and very amusing companion and a most likeable rogue.

Fulke Walwyn obviously thinks so. The great veteran of the Lambourn trainers' guild has, after all, employed Crottie now for so many years he might wince at the memory of how it all started. But Fulke, in common with other trainers, has a special affection for the type of man who brings colour and character to his yard and, despite

As it was then . . . Lambourn High Street in 1932. The building on the right has since been demolished.

As it is now . . . fifty years on, with the new garage forecourt visible on the extreme right.

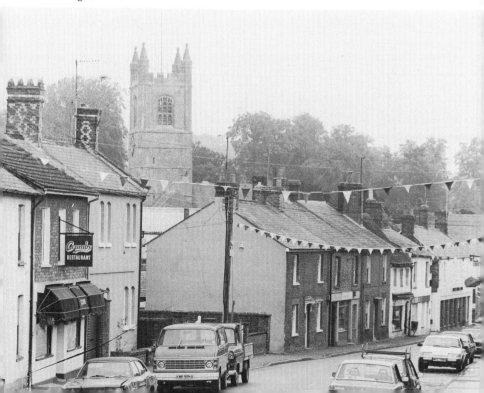

Lambourn from the air, taken in 1929. The downs and the character are unchanged, but most of the wooded area around the church has since been filled in with houses.

The lads of 1921 at Windsor House, now Nicky Henderson's HQ. Hugh Nugent is standing far left, and the burly character standing second from the right is the blacksmith.

Three of Lambourn's best-known characters: *Left:* Trainer Fulke Walwyn, now in his seventies but as ambitious as ever. *Right:* Jockey John Francome, the champion motivated by a new young pretender. *Below:* The incomparable Fred Winter, pictured here when no jockey could match him. Now, as a brilliant trainer, he dreams of his roses.

The lads of yesteryear move off from Windsor House in 1932, with Sir Hugh and Lady Nugent looking on.

The lads of today, not so uniformly smart, reach the downs in the early morning.

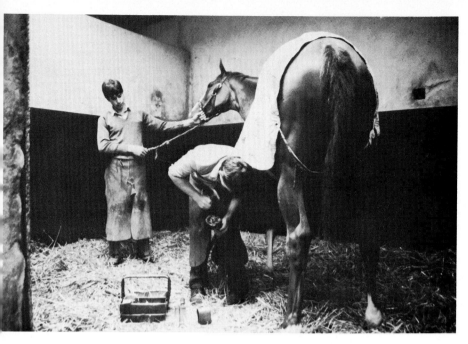

Two of the village's essential craftsmen. *Below :* Resident saddler Cyril 'Blood' Bentick, and *Above :* the local blacksmith at work.

If horses are inseparable from Lambourn, so is betting. Another string passes the focal point of afternoon entertainment.

And, for many, the attraction of each evening: Lambourn's two biggest pubs, side by side in the square.

Left: The road to racing. *Right:* A modern horsebox looks primitive, but ensures that even a frightened horse travels safely.

Supervised by trainer Marcus Marsh (*right*), Windsor Lad leaves his Baydon Road stables before winning the 1934 Derby — Lambourn's first ever success in the greatest flat race of all.

Some things never change: the square and church; the gallops; and the cheerfully phlegmatic lads.

some diverting problems along the way, still knows his duties as a stable-lad and faithfully carries them out.

I met Crottie on a Friday night in 'The Malt'. The usual gathering of lads, chiefly from the yards of Walwyn and Nick Gaselee, had been assembled some while, and a few were showing visible signs of ailing. Crottie made something of a grand entrance, dressed in a dark suit, only slightly crumpled, a white handkerchief protruding from his breast pocket. Raucous as they were by now, the rest of the lads showed due deference and Crottie's stool in the corner of the bar, underneath the calendar and its colour picture of Walwyn's brilliant chaser Diamond Edge, was duly vacated. Squatters' rights, I assumed.

Crottie is not a loud man. Once he had his pint in his hand he set about rolling and smoking an endless chain of cigarettes, the falling ash doing little for the look of his suit. He reminisced quietly, looked forward to the prospects of his own two horses, and the rest of the Walwyn stable. Soon after nine he was ready to go, and I gave him a lift down into the village. The Catholic Club was his next stop – or was it the Legion, I could not quite make him out – and he might have another pint or two before returning home.

It was possible that he might become involved in a game of spoof, as popular among lads as it is among any other group of regular pub-goers, and just as painful to the pocket of the loser who has to buy the next round. But the lads in The Maltshovel were not so keen for Crottie to play with them now. Last time, he would insist on changing his call after the game had started!

But at least he was back in Lambourn. That worry for Fulke Walwyn was over for another winter, although he had probably resigned himself to the same difficulties recurring again and again. For Crottie always returned home during the summer, to his native village in southern Ireland. There, the story goes, he would normally stay until communications were received from Lambourn.

He knew when he was expected back, but the journey was long and expensive, so he lingered in the hope that help might be on the way. And sometimes it was.

The popular tale in Lambourn is that Fulke has frequently sent Crottie his fare to tempt him back again, and ignored the insubordination when he did arrive. But one year, apparently, the fare had been sent and still there was no sign of the little Irishman. So Fulke sent the money again. Still no Crottie.

By chance, a horsebox from the Lambourn transport company was making a trip to Crottie's part of Ireland to collect new inmates for one of the local trainers. Arrangements were made for a slight detour and a personal call at Crottie's home. This ploy did work, and Crottie walked brazenly back into Saxon House, to be told by Mr Walwyn that he was serving notice. The guv'nor's patience was exhausted.

Relations between the two remained strained, at best, in the days which followed and one morning on the gallops, the trainer apparently bawled out Crottie in front of some watching owners. Crottie trotted his horse over to Fulke and said: 'I would like a word with you later, sir.'

He reported to Fulke's office and, on being asked the reason for his request, is said to have replied that Mr Walwyn had being making life so unpleasant for him since he arrived back for the season that he had decided he would not be leaving, notice or no notice.

What Fulke Walwyn's reply was, I am not privileged to know. The story, however, was relayed on good authority and Crottie acknowledged it with a silent smile and a bit more dropping ash. Suffice it to say that he is still there, and the place would not be the same without him.

Wally Lough reported for work before nine o'clock on the morning of Friday, 12 February. As usual, he chattered through his cup of tea in the drivers' rest room at Lambourn Ridgeway Transport's depot, blinding a few of his colleagues with the Irish logic betraying his County Antrim background, and looked forward to the day ahead.

It was a relatively easy day for Wally. The drive to Newbury, for the first day of the traditional Schweppes meeting, involved a round trip of only thirty-two miles and less than two hours' driving time. A far cry from some of the assignments he had been delegated during his two decades as a box driver – the 870-mile Perth run was the most forbidding and unusual, but even Liverpool (392 miles), Doncaster (323 miles) and Bangor-on-Dee (283 miles) required leaving the day before the races concerned and stopping overnight. Newbury, by comparison, was a doddle.

Wally acknowledged, too, that he was one of the lucky guys in regular work. The hard winter had been as harsh on his business as on many others. Three regular drivers and four auxilliaries had all been laid off during January by the company managed by the elegent Jim Cramsie. Even in a normal, uninterrupted National Hunt season, the transport firm budgets for a loss during December and January; current estimates were that, this year, they had lost more than three times the expected figure. If it was not a disaster, it was most certainly a setback. No company could withstand such devasting figures without making cutbacks and Wally was not alone in thanking his God for the return of milder weather.

His duties this particular day were to take three of Nick Gaselee's horses to the meeting. Although the first race was not due off until 1.30, this still involved pulling out of Gaselee's yard by ten o'clock to allow the horses almost three hours to accustom themselves to the change of scene. En route, Wally was instructed to collect a consignment of hay for delivery to the racecourse stables. Four Irish horses were arriving that evening for the following day's racing; this was intended for them.

By 9.30 am, the transport depot was relatively peaceful. The three drivers bound for Newbury had gone. The rest of the boxes were in dock for the day and some of them were being hosed down. One or two drivers relaxed in the rest-room, while in the adjoining offices an accountant pored over figures and Peter, the operations controller, began making plans for the following day.

Half a mile away, Nick Gaselee was finishing his breakfast at Saxon Cottage before driving around the corner in his Land-Rover to supervise the departure of his runners for the day. The regular routine applied; those going racing with the horses would be his travelling head lad, Byron Mills, and the lads responsible for the horses concerned. At 9.58 precisely, Nick swept into his yard, jumped down from the cab and strode through the open-ended barn to where the horsebox was parked. The last of the horses was just being loaded, and within two minutes the journey was underway.

Wally wore a check cap and a blue anorak, along with the suspicion of a smile which twitched at the corners of his mouth throughout the journey. A good, steady driver, he curbed his conversational instinct almost entirely while at the wheel. Alongside him on his front bench seat, David Mooney was hunched low, his hands deep in the pockets of his sleeveless riding jacket. He wore a ring in his left ear and spoke little at first, but my initial impressions of him as a silent type were to be quickly dispelled. Stocky, dark-haired and with a voice suggesting Cockney origins despite the fact that he had lived all his life in Lambourn, Mooney was in charge of Keengaddy, whose eventual target this season was to be the Grand National.

Byron Mills sat nearest the window at the front. A cheery Welshman, flat cap concealing a thinning top, Byron complained that he had been on the road every day for a week and a half. Not that he minded – he later revealed he never knew what to do with himself when there was no racing to attend. Good-naturedly rebuffing the attempted mickey-taking from Mooney, he introduced me to the two lads seated behind me, facing the back of the box and the horses.

Kevin Mancini was a name I knew. He had been considered a promising young rider but a shuddering fall at Plumpton in August 1980 had disturbed his progress. He had broken his jaw and split his jugular vein and doctors told him he might not ride for ten months. He was in fact back on board within three, but had suffered a reduction in rides. He was with Last Argument, a horse highly rated by Gaselee but having his first run for two seasons.

The third horse in the box was an eight-year-old chaser named Mr Gumboots, owned by Mrs Jocelyn Hambro, of life insurance fame. Mr Gumboots' lad was also a lady, although Heidi Dean was at pains to confirm that you could not afford to assume many feminine airs in her job. She wore a colourful woollen hat and sat quietly reading the *Daily Mirror* throughout the journey, after an initial brief commotion when Byron, distributing the petty cash for the day, managed to throw her pay envelope out of the window just as the box pulled out. The short delay was accompanied by resounding laughter from all but Heidi, who scrambled out of the door showing understandable concern for the recapture of this proportion of anything but princely earnings.

Lambourn's old lads, those who have been in the business most of their lives, recall the days when pay packets chinked with nothing much more than a few sixpences and conclude that the modern generation have things easy. Even so, a weekly take-home wage of around £45 has hardly lifted stable-lads into the super-tax bracket. Would they be surly, I wondered? Would they constantly bemoan the level of their existence or the meniality of some of their duties? I need not have worried. The lads I had met and mixed with earlier in the season had given me a fair impression of the phlegmatic, day-to-day lifestyle of their breed, and Messrs Mills, Mooney and Mancini, not to mention Miss Dean, confirmed the notion that racing lads are very happy to make the most of their lot; it is rare indeed to find one eager for change.

Kevin was not yet twenty-three but already seemed an old hand at the game. He had been in the yard for six years, which made him Gaselee's longest-serving lad apart from Mills, who was a founder member. Kevin was busy reminiscing before the box had cleared Lambourn. He told me he had led up the stable's first-ever winner – 'it was also at Newbury, funnily enough, and won by six lengths' – and their hundredth.

Kevin's home was in Warwickshire, only a few miles from mine, and we chatted about common pubs. He lives in digs in Lambourn now but still goes home on his weekend off. 'That's every weekend,' put in David Mooney, mischievously provoking an argument. 'Actually,' said Kevin thoughtfully, 'I usually manage to take my washing home to my mother, but I went in the laundrette in Lambourn last week. It was dreadful – I was in there two hours. Never again.'

At this, more crowing ensued from David, who lives with his parents and has no such problems. 'It won't always be so easy for you,' put in Byron wisely. 'What about when you get married?' Mooney scoffed.

I discovered that both Kevin and David were normally known by nicknames, neither particularly complimentary. Kevin's was 'Eddie'. 'It's short for Eddie headbanger,' he explained, 'because since that fall of mine, everyone in the yard reckons I'm crazy.' Mooney was known as Doris and volunteered the obscure explanation that it originated when his mother made him wear a sweater with buttons down the side during a childhood game of street football. The jibed name had stuck.

'Doris' Mooney still plays football, four times a week on average. He turns out in midfield for Newbury Town, and proudly pointed out their neat, floodlit ground behind a factory as the box nosed its way into town. He also plays for a local Sunday side. Racing might be a job to him, but soccer was a passion, taken so seriously and heatedly that he had collected £35 in disciplinary fines the previous season and had already been sent off during the current term. As we drove on, he pondered what he might do if Newbury were involved in a cup final the day Keengaddy was to run in the Grand National. He had not reached a decision by the time we arrived.

The horses had been silent and apparently disinterested throughout the short journey. I was told that jumpers usually are; flat horses, being better bred, are more temperamental and frequently play up. Kevin's eyes opened wide as he related the story of one such animal which leapt clean out of its partitioned part of the box and tried to escape by the side door. 'A bit frightening,' he said, understandably.

'Most of the horses in our yard are very placid anyway,' said Byron. 'Even you could sit on them and they wouldn't run away with you. Mind you, there is one which plays up a bit. I hit him the other day to calm him down and he went backwards fifty yards. I shan't do that again.'

The box turned into the racecourse approach road, easing over the narrow bridge into the wide parking area next to the stable block. Conversation turned to the races ahead, and tips were freely bandied about. None of the Gaselee horses were likely to be at short odds today, but David quietly fancied his Keengaddy. His elder brother Kevin rides for Fulke Walwyn, and he was also going to bet on one of their runners, Everett.

Wally jumped out to lower the side-gates of the box. The horses were led down one by one while the lads bantered about the prospects of seeing a notorious middle-aged lady of colourful sartorial taste who apparently was well known to the stable staffs of Lambourn. They called her Campari Lil.

Byron, laden with bags and buckets, puffed off to declare the arrival of his runners. No one but stable employees with personal identity cards, is allowed inside the stable block at racecourses. When he returned five minutes later his duties were temporarily done, so we retired to the lads' canteen, an airy room full of café-style tables and chairs and card-schools of the public bar variety. Flat caps abounded and a solitary trilby, the racing headgear of members and owners, looked conspicuous.

The canteen at Newbury is run by Dottie Channing-Williams, landlady of the Five Bells Inn at Wickham. One of her daughters, Karen, was at the counter, and served us with strong, hot tea and well-filled pasties, necessary warming nutrition for a day which, although dry, was growing increasingly chill and blustery.

Most of those who were not playing cards were studying the day's form. The *Sun* and *Mirror* were plainly most popular with the lads. A few *Sporting Lifes* were apparent, but the heavy papers were noticeably absent. Byron, prompted by mention of newspapers, recalled the frequent visits to the yard by Prince Charles over the previous two years. 'We have had two horses for him and he used to come regularly to ride out. He was marvellous, just like one of the lads – and he knew what he was doing, too. But it was bedlam every time he came. The cameramen and journalists overran the place.' He grinned wistfully, for in truth everyone in Gaselee's yard had enjoyed the brief exposure allowed them by the royal visits. There was a touch of regret in Byron's voice as he concluded: 'He has not been back since getting married.'

Byron Mills had accompanied Nick Gaselee when he left Fulke Walwyn's employment in 1976 to set up his own yard. 'I had worked for Mr Walwyn for a number of years but I think they believed I was a jinx on them. The horses I did kept dying, you see. When Mr Gaselee started we had one horse and one lad – me. We've expanded pretty quickly, really.

'One thing I will say about this business. If you're in

racing, you are seldom short of a job. So long as you can do your horses and you are reasonably reliable, there will always be someone to employ you. The wages might not be great, but the lads seem to keep happy. It's brought home to me every time I go home. I come from a mining area in South Wales, near Cardiff, and whenever I go back there seem to be more unemployed blokes from the collieries and steelworks. It's depressing, you know. If my mother didn't live there, I don't think I'd go back at all. I live in a caravan in Mr Gaselee's yard now, and I'm very happy there.'

Heidi was happy, too, although she confessed there had been moments during the first three months of her job when she thought being a stable-lad was maybe not such a good idea for a girl, after all. 'It comes as a shock at first, to be treated just like the boys and to be called all the names under the sun,' she admitted. 'But I developed a tough skin within three months. I can give as good as I get now.'

Brought up in Bath, Heidi was with horses from very early in life and never really wanted to be separated. 'My first job on leaving school was in London, as a nanny. It didn't last long. I'm not cut out to live and work in the city, and I just missed the horses.'

They agreed that the bitter cold weather of December and January was the worst in their combined experience. 'It was miserable,' said Heidi. 'I live a few miles out of Lambourn, and I was up at five in the morning some days, just to defrost my Mini. Even the starter-motor had frozen solid. But it started – which is more than some of the flash new cars in the yard did. Two of my horses are in heated boxes,' she went on. 'But one morning, even in them, the water was frozen in the buckets. When we rode out, just walking them round a straw track, I couldn't even blink because my eyelashes would immediately stick together, frozen solid. I thought I was going to die.'

Byron went off to busy himself, the first race being less than ninety minutes away. I wandered back over the bridge into the street and looked in at The Old London Apprentice. The back bar, or games room, was a haven for thirsty stable-lads, and there were plenty present, quaffing pints and squeezing in a game of pool before hurrying back to make sure their horses were looking a picture.

There is no secret about the pastimes which stable-lads enjoy. They drink, they bet and the younger ones, at least, try to pull the birds. If they can manage all three together, and what's more, while doing a day's work at the races, they are in a seventh heaven.

It was not a memorable day for the Gaselee stable. Last Argument fell at the ninth fence, Keengaddy was pulled up before the last, and Mr Gumboots trailed in thirty lengths behind the penultimate finisher. Nick was far from pleased. In a voice I took to be only partly jesting he said midway through the afternoon: 'You don't seem to have brought us much luck.' Knowing the superstitions of people in racing, I wondered how many might genuinely have blamed me!

The lads were late back to the box at the end of racing. Everett had won, and after collecting their winnings, they had celebrated with tea and a bite to eat in the lads' canteen. Wally sat patiently at the wheel of his cabin, chatting reflectively about the thirty-two years since he first came to work in England, the people he had met, the races he had seen, the horses he had carried. Been about a bit, had Wally.

Finally, we were off, weaving through the obstacle course of rival boxes and horses, David exchanging fatuous waves with lads from other stables, Kevin wondering how quickly his horse would run again and give him another day out, Heidi silent again in the corner.

It was rush-hour in Newbury. A striking young lady in a Ford pulled out on to a roundabout in front of the box, then threw up her arm in mock terror as Wally's wagon advanced on her. It was slow progress out of town, but not slow enough for the lads. After such a disappointing day, they expected the guv'nor might not be at his cheeriest at evening stables, and were in no rush to find out. Even so, the journey took only half an hour. Dusk was falling fast and spots of rain were punctuating the windscreen as we pulled up at the yard. At once, the welcoming party advanced; the lads who had been left behind wanted full details of the day, and a dozen questions were asked at once. Byron began to answer but they got little sense out of David or Kevin. The day's work was almost done. There was now a Friday night in the pub to look forward to.

Wally Lough turned the empty box round and headed back to the depot. It was raining hard now, and would continue all night. But Wally didn't mind. He was still smiling. 'Those young lads,' he said. 'They're barmy, I'm sure.'

7·Lambourn Ladies

JENNY Pitman has a stentorian voice and a slightly intimidating appearance. Necessary accessories, perhaps, for one who has made a success of training racehorses in Lambourn despite the starting-price handicap of being a woman. I say that without any intention of sexism. The fact is that training is thought to be a man's domain and Lambourn is thought, by most people anyway, to be a man's village. So maybe it was not surprising that I heard Mrs Pitman described in tones which combined suspicion with cynicism. To make things worse, so far as the bulk of Lambourn's training populace is concerned, Jenny has the drawback of being unsociable. She admits as much. 'We never see her,' said one trainer. 'She calls us the gin and tonic set and can't understand that we enjoy each other's company in the evenings.'

So, as one who qualifies on two counts as being in the opposing camp – I am male and I enjoy a gin and tonic – it was with some trepidation that I kept my appointment at Weathercock House in Upper Lambourn on the morning of the Schweppes Hurdle at Newbury. It was a warm, sunny day, the misery of the snows seemed remote, and Jenny was marching past her stable boxes as I drove in. She was dressed in sweater and trousers and yelled across to me to proceed into the house. I picked a path around various pets and found myself in a cosy lounge decorated with hunting prints, horse miniatures and the mandatory video set – no different, in fact, to the great majority of trainer's lounges I had visited in preceding months.

Jenny arrived presently, bearing coffee. She is a well-built lady, with fair hair, and when she smiles the feeling is infectious. I began to like her. We sat for more than an hour, talking about her life, and I left with a vivid impression of a girl who has beaten considerable odds by doing things in her own particular, sometimes dogmatic, way. She may not have been qualified to lecture in winning friends and influencing people – but she had won enough, and influenced enough, to build a substantial business and secure its survival in an unkind economic climate.

She had suffered a broken marriage, to former jockey turned television racing man Richard Pitman, and a number of other personal hardships and setbacks. They had, paradoxically, done her some good, she reckoned. 'I've been toughened up,' she said. 'You have to learn to live with the kicks in this life, and not dwell on the disappointments. I used to cry very easily, I was soft and vulnerable. I wouldn't say I was as hard as iron now, but I can cope . . .

'Sometimes, things can really shatter you in this game. We had three winners at a televised meeting at Worcester one Saturday – the first and so far only time I have done that. The very next week, at Sandown, one of the winners, Roll of Drums, dropped dead during a race. It takes a tough person to smile bravely and shrug that off. Yes, I cried a bit.'

Jenny effectively began training horses when she was fourteen and living on her parents' farm in Leicestershire. While still at school she 'trained' her father's point-to-pointer. 'He would tell me to gallop him five times around the field at home,' she recalled. 'But I used to give him two and a half circuits, then let him have a rest because he was tired. It wasn't surprising that he didn't win much! We always had ponies on the farm, but I didn't get much opportunity to ride them. Eventually, Dad gave me the chance to ride our horse in a point-to-point. I shall never forget it. We fell at the fifth, and I was a bit shaken up. But when I looked up, lying there on the mud feeling groggy, I saw a St John's Ambulance man running towards me with his bag open. I jumped up and hurried back to the changing-rooms. I was a real tomboy, and I wasn't going to stand for him examining me.'

Jenny left school at fifteen and started work for her father. 'I was paid £3 4s. 5d. a week. I gave my Mum thirty bob and saved ten bob. That meant I had exactly £1 4s. 5d. to spend – and I had it worked out down to the last penny.'

Her first racing job was for trainer Chris Taylor, at Bishop's Cleeve, near Cheltenham. 'I was still fifteen when I went there, and I was very homesick. I suppose every kid of that age would be the same, leaving home for the first time. But I got over it all right, and when I was offered a job in Lambourn, in Major Champniss's yard, I had very few doubts about taking it.'

She joined the Champniss yard as a stable-girl, doing her two horses. But not before an eventful exit from Bishop's Cleeve which still makes her giggle now. 'I had a little Ford Popular in those days, which was not the most reliable of vehicles. I piled all my belongings in there, plus my dog, and we set off for Lambourn. But on the way out of Bishop's Cleeve there is a steep hill, and the car boiled up. We had only got about a mile and I thought that was my lot. But by driving very slowly, we managed to limp into Lambourn and settle into the caravan which was to be my home.'

Jenny married Richard when she was eighteen. Within two months she was pregnant. 'We lived in the cottage where Nick Gaselee is now – but it was a bit different in those days. There was no sanitation and no hot water, but we didn't mind because we were in love and you put up with a lot for that. I left Major Champniss just before Christmas, because I didn't want him to give me another present. Silly really, because he did anyway. Richard and I bought a bungalow in the village and I had to get used to the idea of having a kid. It was a shock, because I had never so much as looked after one before. It was lucky I even managed to feed him at the right end. Richard had started to get more rides, but he was still on the way up. He only earned £14 a week, and when we went into supermarkets we had to keep counting our money to make sure we had enough. Habits stick, you know, because I still do that now . . .'

It was, so far, a common enough tale of a young married couple battling to keep their heads above water. The Pitmans moved to Hinton Parva, a hamlet between Lambourn and Swindon, and Jenny was soon expecting their second child. 'By the time we had been married two years, I had two sons,' she says. 'Of course, it changed my life. I was virtually inactive as far as horses were concerned, although I did find the time to train some point-to-pointers at Hinton Parva.'

In 1977 the Pitmans separated and Jenny had to decide what to do with her life. Her first move was back into Lambourn, to Weathercock House in fact. But the neat, well-scrubbed, almost affluent look of the place today gives a false impression. 'It was,' Jenny explains, 'like a horror movie when I first saw it. It had been on the market a long time, and when I came to look at it I could see why. There was no real access from the road, and there were holes in the roof. But they were just the obvious things from the outside. When I came inside there were cobwebs round all the windows and thick layers of dust on the floor. Worst of all, there were metal rat-traps in the kitchen – and I am even terrified of mice. The asking price was £30,000. I offered £18,000 and they couldn't believe my cheek. But I eventually bought it for £25,000. When we began work, it was all very daunting. We started on the dust, and couldn't see each other from one side of the room to the other. I asked Norman Francome, John's father and a builder, to come and look at the roof for me, and he fell through the stairs. But gradually, we started to get things straight.'

Training was not at first on the agenda. 'But I had been

quite successful with a point-to-point horse for a man called Tony Stratton-Smith, and he got in touch and asked me if I would train his racehorses. It was a difficult decision because it meant starting right at the bottom of the pile. But I agreed to give it a go.'

It was unusual for a woman to venture into training, although by no means unknown. What was unknown was for any female to achieve a success parallel to their male counterparts. Jenny Pitman broke through, but it was no instant success.

'Richard came back to live at the house for a while, and we gave it another try. But it was not going to work, and when he left for the last time, I had only nine horses, and things looked a bit grim. The male dominance had never bothered me, because I always thought I could do the job as well as any of them. They teased me, of course, but I received a lot of support from men like David Nicholson and Fred Winter, and a few words of kindness meant a great deal to me.'

There were twenty-five horses in training at Weather-cock House the day I called, and very few of them were unlikely to win a race. What is more, the family side of Jenny Pitman's life had resolved itself happily. Her two sons were growing up – Mark, now fifteen, was about to leave school and work for David Nicholson at Stow; fourteen-year-old Paul wanted to be an accountant. 'They come home for their Sunday lunch, and we all look forward to that,' says Jenny. 'You see, I live in Lambourn for the purpose of training National Hunt horses, because there is nowhere in England to rival it. I would not say I am in love with the place, and I don't get involved in the social set of trainers because I don't want to. But I enjoy my life.'

When she was a little girl, far too young to go into pubs, Di Dearie was sometimes taken by her parents to The Maltshovel in Upper Lambourn, and sat on the grass with a lemonade and a bag of crisps. The days of her memory were all warm and sunny, and her impressions of the pub were confined to childlike notions of what must go on inside, coupled with a passing fascination for the small, flat-capped figures who passed in and out of the door with regularity. The one idea which never occurred to her was that, one day, she might run the pub herself and become not only a provider of beer, but a friend and confidante to the flat-capped figures and their successors.

If one could draw a mental picture of the landlady in a Lambourn racing pub, Di would fit most of the requirements very adequately. She has the type of smiling face you feel instinctively you can trust, she wears comfortable country clothes and she chats in easy, friendly fashion without interrogating. The lads in The Maltshovel love her, and not without good reason.

'The Malt' was a seventeenth-century bakehouse. But for many years now it has been a local to the stable-lads at several Upper Lambourn yards, most notably those of Fulke Walwyn and Nick Gaselee. It has old beams, scrubbed floorboards and character, but is neither posh nor plush. None of its regulars would want that, and neither would Di. 'Don't make this place out to be posh, whatever you do,' she pleaded when we talked one morning just after opening time. She had just finished her daily chore of cleaning the insides of the windows after their coating of smoke the previous night. Stable-lads tend to enjoy a cigarette as well as a pint, and it does glass no good at all. Di was dressed in a Parka jacket and skirt and she managed to deal with the handful of early-morning thirsts while we talked.

Behind her, Tommy Dearie studied the racing papers, glasses perched on his nose and an intent frown creasing his features. Tommy, Di's husband, went into racing at fourteen, served his apprenticeship with trainer Bill Elsey in Malton, and then rode on the flat until he broke his spine. He comes from Ayr and has never really settled in Lambourn. Di says he hankers after a home in Minorca, where he regularly holidays. Give Tommy any encouragement and he will produce his scrapbooks and photographs depicting his riding career. He remains totally immersed in the sport, and although his involvement these days is restricted to reminiscing and punting, he retains his enthusiasm. Di, with no hint of malice, laughs: 'If I took ill and passed out in here, Tommy would step over me to get the racing results.'

Di herself is not devoid of a racing background. Her father, a Cockney, was a jockey, as were her uncle and grandfather. But her grandmother went into the pub trade, and it was through her, perhaps, that the idea was born in Di's mind. 'We started to look for a place round here while Tommy was still riding, and I remembered this pub from coming here as a girl. It happened to become available and we took it over in 1960. We were under no illusions about the type of pub it was – we both knew a fair bit about Lambourn, and as my parents still lived here I had friends in the area. The difficult thing was that neither Tommy nor I had ever stood behind a bar. For the first few weeks, I used to go and hide out the back whenever I could see a big round coming up. I just couldn't face the thought of getting it all wrong. But nobody seemed to mind.'

The Maltshovel's custom consists of a few regular locals, chiefly retired gentlemen who come in early at lunchtime for their beer, and a great deal of racing lads. Seldom can any pub, anywhere, have been so dominated by one trade. But Di doesn't mind. 'Racing lads must be the happiest folk in the world,' she says. 'They never have much money, and sometimes they have none at all once they've had a drink. But I could count on the fingers of one hand the number of times I have seen any of them miserable. I suppose it's because they like their job so much – they must or they wouldn't do it for the money they get paid. But I'm glad they are our customers. The great thing is, I could call on any of them to help out with the bar. When Tommy is away, they often do the barrels for me. Nothing is ever too much trouble.'

Di's day starts at eight o'clock, and sometimes rather slowly if the boys have been in good drinking form the previous night. She has a regular quota of morning jobs to do. 'But I must admit I'm a bit of a chatterbox, and the work sometimes gets behind. We never know when we are going to be busy, and as we are only a small pub and have no outside staff, the workload for Tommy and I can vary enormously. The lads generally finish for lunch at about midday, and come in here pretty soon afterwards, so by half-past twelve there is a good crowd in. Some lads come in here every lunchtime and almost every evening,' she claimed, turning for support to one who was ordering his first pint of the day. He confirmed that he had worked in Lambourn for sixteen years and could not remember the last day on which a visit to 'The Malt' had been over-looked.

'It's a way of life for them,' went on Di. 'More of a club than a pub. They all meet in here and chat about their yards and their horses, and what is going to win to-morrow. In the evenings, they might only come in for a couple before going out somewhere else – but they rarely miss out completely. Our busiest days are when the weather is very bad and there is no racing. The lads finish early and come in straight away. They also tend to stay longer.'

One of the daily regulars is Fulke Walwyn's enigmatic veteran lad, Paddy Crottie. From his stool in the corner of the bar, he will hold court in that curious tongue which sounds Irish, yet is more difficult to understand. 'Crottie says things backwards, I am sure,' said Di. 'I never can make out what he is saying. But he's got a good heart, you know, and I am sure he will be remembered around Lambourn long after most of us are forgotten.'

By now, it was past midday, and the bar was filling up with flat caps and form tips. 'People come here for the first time and listen to all the information being bandied around, thinking it must be easy to make a fortune,' said Di. 'But I wouldn't be standing behind here if it was easy – and neither would most of the lads be standing there.'

It suddenly struck me that there was not a single girl in the pub. Di nodded. 'That is one thing we are short of,' she smiled. 'We do get the occasional stable-girl in, but then the lads are like bees around a honeypot.'

Di took an order for a few pints and battled with the mental arithmetic. 'It's a good job I don't work in a bank. I'm terrible with figures. Last week, I managed to mis-place £1,000 in our accounts, somehow.' It was becoming hectic, so I said my goodbyes, returned the banter of the livelier lads and prepared to leave. Di smiled indulgently at yet another cheeky remark in her direction. 'They are good fun,' she said. 'Now and again they want a shoulder to cry on and they tell me all their troubles. I think they like me after all this time. It's funny, me ending up as a landlady in a place like this. I always wanted to be a nurse.'

Seven o'clock on a Friday night and Marje Morrow was not at her best. She had just woken from a recuperative early-evening sleep, and lit a cigarette as she sat back in her armchair, a half-full bottle of Lucozade at her side. Thursday night had been late and hectic and she had not yet fully recovered. It would not have been so bad, but as usual she had been up at five in the morning, working half-an-hour later. I shuddered at the thought.

Everyone knows Marje. She runs the papershop, Cripps', and her face and smile are as much a part of a Lambourn morning as the clip-clopping of Barry Hills' string walking through the square. Divorced and in her early fifties, Marje has the flat above the shop. To reach her cosy front room, which overlooks The George and no doubt many a vivid night-time sight, you walk down a corridor past stacks of newspapers. This is the order area, where the deliveries are sorted each morning at a time when only the most conscientious or insomniac stable-lads are about. Then it is up a winding flight of stairs to a self-contained flat. It wasn't always so. 'When I moved in,' Marje recalls, 'this was a one-room bedsit. A contracted company sorted the papers each morning in the next room, where my kitchen is now. I used to lie in bed, jumping at every thump as another parcel of papers was thrown down.'

Marje moved to Lambourn twenty-one years ago, but she has only been based at the shop since 1970. Originally from Swindon, she has two daughters, one of whom forms a close link with Lambourn racing via her marriage to Peter Walwyn's head lad. Her first impressions of Lambourn were not encouraging. 'I came through the place once when I took part in a motor rally. I remember thinking what a weird town it was, full of little men standing on street corners.' I recalled immediately thinking exactly the same myself! 'Of course, when I came to live here, I soon worked out they were just hanging about between listening to races in the betting shop. But it does look odd, doesn't it?'

Adjusting to the men on the corners was not Marje's only problem on coming to live in the village. She found herself threatened with being an outcast, because she knew nothing of racing and had never thought much of night life. 'It took me years to work out that there was a difference between flat racing and jump racing. But it got through to me that I had to develop an interest, or I would become a cabbage. When I came to Lambourn, I had never been in a pub, never even had a drink. It might sound funny, but I hadn't. But I realized that unless I went in the pubs I would not meet anybody. There is a big difference between people who come in the shop and people you can call friends.'

Marje began to go into The George, and was befriended by Noël Bennett, then the landlord. It was probably, without exaggeration, the turning-point in her life. 'I missed cooking for a family,' she explains. 'My daughters had moved on – there was only me here. So every Sunday I would see Noël and say: "How many for lunch?" He would probably say about ten and I would cook for five extra. I enjoyed those days.'

The Red Lion is Marje's local now. She worked there as a barmaid for a time, some years back, and was a colleague of Flo, who has been working in the late-night back bar for more years than anyone cares to remember. Even now, Marje could not be called a hardened drinker, but The Red Lion is open until two every morning, everyone is friendly and she naturally inherits the occasional headache. Such as the specimen she was suffering as we talked. 'People who come into a Lambourn pub for the first time are amazed at the size of the rounds,' she says. 'Maybe it means we are a particularly sociable community, but as soon as you are accepted, you become part of everyone's round.'

Marje opens the doors of Cripps' at 6.30 each morning. Most of her paper boys are at school, of course, and they cannot legally be dispatched on their rounds until seven. They also have to catch a school bus at eight, so few of them have more than forty houses on their delivery list. 'The trainers all have the *Sporting Life*,' she says, 'and generally one or two other papers. The *Daily Telegraph* is popular. But most of the racing lads come in to buy their own papers, and not many of them can afford to have the *Life* every day now. They will take it for the major meetings, or when one of their horses is fancied – I always know, you see – but otherwise they will get by with one of the pop papers. I sell more of the *Sun* than anything else. Most of the lads smoke, and I have come to know which cigarettes each of them will ask for in the morning. But the thing they buy most of is sweets. Almost without exception, they have sweet teeth. They won't just buy one bar of chocolate – it will be three or four. I suppose it must give them energy. They hate debts, the lads. They might not get paid much, but they are very proud. Every now and again, one of them will be 2p or 3p short, and I will tell him to pay me the next day. Nine times out of ten I'll forget, but they never do.'

It would be very misleading to suggest that all Marje's custom is from the racing profession. A great many are housewives, and some of those come from the new estates where racing is a word associated only with television on a Saturday afternoon and 'those dirty horses walking past outside again'. Marje, who has soft, comfortable eyes and a benign smile, is as sympathetic to them as she is to the majority interests in the village. 'Lots of the women who come in are scared of the horses,' she says. 'I am not talking about the type who have just moved into the village and start complaining immediately – they should have known what they were coming to, and I have no time for their moans. But a lot of real locals are frightened of the enormous strings which you can see on the roads some mornings. The flat horses, especially, can be temperamental, and it would only take one of them to get upset and a child in a pushchair could be badly hurt. I think the strings are too long, and could be better regulated.'

Marje was well awake now, and was talking of having a bath before walking across to The Red Lion. It was Friday night, after all.

'There is no age barrier here, that's what I like about the place. And no class system, either. Everyone talks to everyone else. I see them all in the shop, but they are only people, after all. Jockeys like John Francome come in regularly for a chat – and I like John a lot, because on the rare occasions when I go racing, he will always pick me out and say hallo, no matter who he is with. That's the spirit of this village. People don't care what you are doing here. You might hear a bit of gossip about someone, and of course you are interested. But you don't think the person concerned is any better or worse for it.'

Sandra Bentick is very clearly the daughter of saddler Cyril. Her hair may not be quite so blood-red as her father's, but the similarity is enough for identification purposes. There is a hint of freckles on her face and she smiles in that infectious style which characterizes, for some odd reason, most redheads.

Just like Cyril in his sweet-smelling workshop, Sandra is happy in her work as a trainer's secretary. Surprisingly, perhaps, it was what she always wanted to do from junior school age. But, also like Cyril, there is a frustration still gnawing at her in her job. Cyril would love to have trained a winner. Sandra would love to have ridden one. That the nearest either came to realizing the ambition was a runner-up at Stratford is no condemnation of their ability, for in truth their resources were slender when Cyril trained as a permit-holder and Sandra did the work-riding and race-riding. It was a family operation and success was strictly in the bonus bracket.

Sandra went to work for Nicky Henderson in September of 1981, just as he was organizing his first runners of the new season. The job was anything but strange to her, after nine years in the hurly-burly of Peter Walwyn's office. That was flat racing, which made for hectic summers; this was jump racing and now the winters would be her busy seasons. Otherwise, the routine was much the same.

It had, of course, been Cyril who encouraged Sandra into racing. 'I had a pony when I was eight years old, and, having always lived in Lambourn, it was natural that I should develop a love for horses. Dad mentioned one day that I should try to become a trainer's secretary because it would mean I could spend my life with horses. I adopted the idea and never really thought about doing anything from that day on. At the back of my mind was the thought that I might pick up some rides, being on the spot all the time. But in nine years at Walwyn's I only had two rides on the flat and I resigned myself to accepting that there would be no more. Nick's secretary was leaving and he asked me if I would like to join him. A jumping yard was a change, and fresh opportunities, so I came.'

Another characteristic of the redhead brigade is tenacity, and Sandra had certainly not given up the notion of resuming her riding. All season she waited, patiently and uncomplainingly entering up the Henderson horses and declaring the jockeys. Then, in early May, it happened: 'Nick said he would put me up on a horse called Victory Hymn, a six-year-old novice hurdler. I shan't pretend I wasn't excited. I climbed up into our loft at home and fetched the saddles from where they had been stored. I went for a run to get a bit fitter. Then a few days before the race, Nick told me the horse had chipped a bone and was out for the season. It was a big disappointment, but I have left my saddles out, just in hope.'

Sandra sat at her desk in the neat little office, attached to the bulk of Windsor House and looking out on the yard which was once owned and operated by Sir Hugh Nugent. In front of her was a modern telephone with a panel of buttons and lights for the various extension lines. She was flicking through a box-file full of cards on which the entries and performances of each of the yard's horses was entered. It was mid morning and around Lambourn, in more than thirty other stableyard offices, something similar was happening.

A healthy proportion of racing secretaries are female, and this is one area in which they certainly suffer from no jibes of inferiority. Fred Winter, however, has for some seasons been served by a gentleman of the military background which seems to typify so many racing stewards. Lawrence Eliott, a 63-year-old bachelor son of a colonel, does not fall into the category of self-important bore. He has a wry sense of humour and is fortunate, not to say resilient, to have any humour left in him at all, having been a Japanese prisoner-of-war for four years and an inmate of the infamous Changi jail. He came into racing virtually by accident through a friendship with Dick Hern and his wife. They persuaded him to try his hand at secretaryship and, via Bob Turnell, he arrived at Uplands where he now administers Fred Winter's paperwork and fields enquiries from all comers with the patient politeness of a diplomat.

In essence the routines of Sandra and Lawrence are very similar, but there is one difference – an important one, too, to Sandra, who arrives at Windsor House each morning at 7.30 to ride out with the first lot. Lawrence has no inclination to be aboard a racehorse at such an hour. Soon after nine, Sandra is in the office for the most hectic hour of the day. 'I used to have a break for breakfast after riding out. But the deadline for withdrawing horses declared for the following day's meetings has been brought forward an hour to ten o'clock, so there is no time to spare now. It is absolute bedlam in here for that hour. I generally phone up the courses where we are due to have runners, to check the going. Once Nick has made up his mind, sometimes after talking with the owner, I make the calls to get the horses out we don't want to run. Then I might have time to grab some breakfast.'

It is Sandra who communicates regularly with the blacksmith, the transport company and, when necessary, the dentist and the vet. Her voice has become so familiar to these vital cogs of the Lambourn machine that she seldom has to introduce herself on the phone nowadays. After ten years as a trainers' secretary, you expect to be known.

Some days are set aside for specific tasks. Tuesdays, for instance are always taken up by entering the horses. Not only does the list have to be compiled and delivered to John Rodbourn, over the road in Hungerford Hill, for the courier service to Wellingborough, but also the diary has to be completed, each horse's card brought up to date, and postcards sent to each of the stable's owners with details of their horses' entries. 'Towards the end of the week I start on the bookkeeping, and then there are the wages to do,' says Sandra. 'In the winter, when racing is very busy, I might be here from 7.30 in the morning until 6.30 at night, but I don't mind that. It is enjoyable work. We have very friendly owners so it is rarely a problem having to deal with their enquiries – but some of them do appear to think I should know what every horse in the yard is doing at that particular moment,' she adds with a freckled grin.

Sandra lived with her parents while she was single and had no desire to move out of Lambourn when she married Nick Henderson's former second jockey Jimmy Nolan in July. They had already bought a cottage in the village, in fact. She had no wish to change her job either. 'I have loved every minute of being a secretary,' she insisted, adding wistfully, 'with the one regret being the lack of rides.'

It was the day before the flat season began, and to celebrate the village was dressed up in its summer clothes. The lads had discarded their jackets and caps, the young wives had donned bright dresses. The sun shone all day from a hazy blue sky which evoked thoughts of June . . . but it was only 24 March, jump racing had ten weeks still to run and today, the earthy sporting pleasures could be found at three singularly unromantic spots.

'Kelso, Southwell and Worcester,' repeated Sue Hawkins with some distaste as she pinned up the *Sporting Life* form guides in Ladbroke's betting shop. 'It's very bad racing today, so we might not get too busy. Most people will be saving their money for tomorrow, you see.'

Sue has pretty features, long dark hair and a good dress sense. She wears a necklace proclaiming her name, and is as far removed from the common conception of a betting-shop manager as it is possible to be. But manager she is, and very good at it too, judging by my day of observation in one of Lambourn's most popular attractions. For if the village's male working population like a drink and a girl, as the widely-held theory insists, it is a moot point whether a bet is the most indispensable feature in their way of life.

Surprisingly, it was only three years ago that Ladbroke's moved into Lambourn, taking over the shop from an American company, who had previously bought it from a local man whose eye for a thriving business turned his kitchen into a betting office. At one time, Lambourn had two operating betting offices, separated by a few yards in the same road. Now all the trade, and there is plenty of it, comes to one place, but not all of it finds its way to the counter which Sue Hawkins and her staff operate.

I had not been long in Lambourn before I discovered the rival to Ladbroke's. It is a one-man operation of bizarre proportions. The gentleman concerned stands outside the door of the Ladbroke's office six days a week, come rain, snow or sun, and with a beguiling absence of shame, peels off plenty of the official business. His methods are simple. He listens to the odds for each race through either the small, high window or the air vent. Then he may slightly improve upon them for his customers. Sue Hawkins is philosophically resigned to this illicit opposition. 'He stands out there in all weather and people might think he's mad. I reckon he makes a fortune. He is suspicious of strangers, but he has his regular customers among the locals, and there is not much we can do about it. We can't have our door open, as that would make it too easy for him. But he has the cheek of the devil, you know. He waves cheerily at us through the window every morning, and gets really upset if we ignore him.'

He did not look a gambling mogul, leaning on the drainpipe in grubby anorak and jeans, tatty *Sporting Life* in one hand and cigarette in the other. But I met him again two nights later, in a local pub, and both his sharp suit and manner betrayed the fact that he had made a bob or two out of his dealings.

On the morning of the 24 March, however, I was at Ladbroke's before the opposition. Sue, who had been manager for only five months but had worked in village betting businesses for seven years, had arrived at her usual hour, shortly before ten. She sorted out the till, brought the outstanding paperwork up to date, pinned the relevant papers around the walls and switched on the six video screens which show the prices and results throughout the afternoon. She opened the door of the shop at 10.15 a.m. and did not exactly have to step back smartly to avoid the rush.

For an hour or more there was no smoke, no noise and precious little action in the L-shaped betting hall. The videos flashed up diverting snippets, such as the fact that Lambourn's John Francome was locked at 93 winners apiece with his great rival Peter Scudamore at the head of the Jockeys' Championship. Both were engaged at Worcester, the best of the afternoon's three moderate meetings, but at this early hour it seemed the punting public of Lambourn were intent on keeping their hard-earned cash in their pockets.

Of those who did venture over the threshold, most seemed to be retired and a surprising number were women. They were regulars every day, Sue assured me, and although they scarcely qualified for help as hardened gamblers, they each enjoyed their flutter to a certain formula. 'It's like an outing for the old ladies who come in,' she explained. 'If you aren't directly involved in racing, there isn't much to do in Lambourn, and this is their way of keeping an interest in what goes on.'

Sue had a word and a smile for them all. She knew them by name, every one of them, and seemed surprised when I commented on this. 'I know virtually every customer,' she said. 'I might not know everything about them, but I know their faces, in most cases their names, and very often exactly what type of bet they will have. That gentleman round the corner, for instance,' she added, indicating her subject with a toss of her head, 'will have a 25p yankee. He does the same every day. It makes the job more fun when you know the customers and can have a conversation with them. It gets to the stage when I start to worry if I see a strange face in here, like yours the other day . . .'

Sue was born in Lambourn, but moved away at an early age. She returned at eighteen and got married. Her husband is a builder and they live with their two children in a terraced house just behind the church. 'You could say I've got latch-key kids, I suppose, because I am always still at work when they come home from school. But they are well looked after by one of the neighbours. My work is a little unpredictable, but most weeks I will do fifty hours. I am paid to do a job, and I do it until it's finished,' she added with a certain pride. 'Like most people round here, I have connections in racing. My grandfather and uncle were both blacksmiths, so I was always interested in the sport. I get to Newbury every now and again, but I prefer flat racing to jumping – which puts me in a minority in these parts.'

It was approaching midday and Sue knew that the lull would soon be over. 'The racing lads finish about this time, and they aren't due back at their stables until half-past four. Most of them go and have a drink in one of the pubs – normally The Red Lion, The Lamb or The Maltshovel – and then come in here. Some of them won't bet much at all – if they do have a bet it will only be a pound or two out of interest – but they will join in all the debating on which horse is going to win. It's more like a social club than a betting shop, sometimes. The lads are wicked, you know. They really tease me and play all kinds of tricks. It doesn't worry me – in fact I enjoy it – because I'm the out-going sort, and like chatting and meeting people and having some fun. But one of the other girls who worked here found the boys very difficult to cope with.

'Some of the older lads are great characters,' she went on, and I knew Harry Foster was about to be mentioned. 'Harry will bet in spasms. He will come in every day for a week, putting on quite big amounts, and then he'll find it hurting his pocket and you won't see him in the shop, but you might run across him in a pub, telling everyone who cares to listen that gambling is a mug's game. You can't argue with Harry, though.'

As I sat one side of the counter, and Sue stood on the other, separated by that impersonal but essential grille found in so many betting offices, there was still a steady trickle of pensioner punters. 'During the afternoons,' said Sue, 'the only people who spend much time in here are lads and pensioners. But in the mornings, we get all types. Women come in here with their kids before racing starts. We wouldn't allow it later in the day, but it doesn't matter when there is nobody here. I am amazed at the patterns in which people bet. There is one old girl who only ever comes into back horses trained by Ray Laing, for instance.'

Help had arrived in the shape of a middle-aged, bespectacled lady from Newbury, a relief for Sue's regular assistant who was on a day off. She settled down to the *Daily Telegraph* crossword, but not before informing me that she much preferred working in the Lambourn shop. 'People are much friendlier here, probably because they are directly involved with the racing. There is a good atmosphere,' she said.

When I left for lunch, only three customers were present: an old boy who mumbled incomprehensibly as he peered at the form details through thick glasses; a gentleman dressed entirely in country tweeds; and yet another in the stream of women with their yankees, patents and pinstickers. The lads' invasion was not yet underway.

An hour later, the place had begun to buzz. Half a dozen men who wore the look of regulars were earnestly poring over their betting slips; the opposition layer had arrived and stationed himself by the air vent for the first race from Worcester; Sue's assistant had been forced to lay down her crossword and take some money.

'There used to be times when you could hardly get through the door here,' recalled Sue. 'But in those days, we used to take bets on board prices, which meant the lads who thought they had a good thing from their yard running could get the first price available before the on-course money ruined the odds. We stopped that a few years ago, and some of the interest went with it. Even so, it is very hard to predict just when we will be busy. Some days I am sure it will be quiet and I bring a book to read, only to find I never even pick it up because it's so hectic. Other days I look at the card and think we are bound to be rushed off our feet and things never get going at all. The trouble is, even on quiet days, I don't get the long periods in which I could really catch up with things. As soon as I think I am on top of the job, someone comes in and starts chatting, and that is ten minutes gone. They tell me all their secrets here, you see, and you've got to be friendly in a job like this, haven't you?'

It is now ten minutes before the off, but Worcester's opener, a novice hurdle, is attracting minimal interest from the punters. 'We'll be off tomorrow,' one says, obviously relishing the summer sport, 'and I suppose we'll all be backing Barry Hills again.' He then returns to quiet consideration of the Worcester runners and plumps for the favourite, trained in the north by Michael Dickinson. It is beaten by an outsider, ridden by the local boy John Francome. No one in the shop has backed him. 'He must have fed it fish and chips,' mutters one disgruntled customer cryptically. 'Still, he can win us something later on.'

There is, clearly, hope of a 'nice touch' to come. In the 4 p.m. at Worcester, Francome rides Sharp Deal, trained at Windsor House by Nicky Henderson. The inhabitants of Ladbrokes are confident of collecting on this one. There had even been a whisper for the horse the previous day – I had heard a couple of lads discussing it in The George. It happens a few times each week; the word goes around the village that a horse is fancied, and the queue forms at Ladbroke's. Some they win, some they lose.

The shop is still not packed, by any stretch of the imagination. But they are pleasantly busy, and the characters who are to stay the distance and remain there all afternoon are by now apparent. There is an odd, seedy little man with no humility, who reckons he backs every winner and announces it with an irritating nonchalance; there is an old chap with a flat hat who sits in the corner, smiles, and makes the odd cheery remark to anyone who cares to listen; there is a man in his thirties, dressed incongruously smartly in velvet jacket and cream slacks, spending an inordinate time filling out his betting slips as he studies the *Sporting Life*; and there is a stocky, slightly intimidating sort with paint on his trousers and a Wrangler sweatshirt worn back to front. Altogether, something of a motley crew, but they are fixtures while others flit in and out.

Sharp Deal runs prominently, and the corner flat cap keeps repeating his name with a tone of confidence. He is beaten into fourth place, though, and an air of aggrieved silence settles over the place. Finally, someone says, 'He let us down there,' and I was left to work out just who he was referring to.

A thick mist of smoke hangs over the room now. Sue and her assistant work steadily, but not frantically, and the customers, who seem not to have had a profitable after- noon, contemplate possible sources of recouping. The racing lads head back to their stables, the pensioners wander off for their tea and their nap. The opposition man still leans on the drainpipe outside, a couple of cronies at his elbow. I headed for the fresh air. It was just another day for the punting population of Lambourn, after all.

8·Parish Matters

THE Church bells were chiming as I stopped the car opposite The Red Lion. It was a Thursday evening, bell-ringing practice I assumed, and I wondered idly as I pulled up my overcoat collar if the exercise gave them any insulation against weather of this sort.

Valentine's Day had just passed, Cheltenham was still a month away. It was, in fact, the time of year when even romantic souls tend to deflate. Show me someone who enjoys mid-February, and I will show you a masochist. The persistent pealing apart, Lambourn was peaceful. Only a scattering of early quaffers were in the front bar of The Red Lion preparing for the usual Thursday night disco. The George was deserted and the square was still and silent. But further down the Wantage Road, a regular trickle of cars were pulling up and unloading. The occupants, a baker's dozen in all, marched purposefully across the street and through the door of a building which I had often mistaken for a public convenience – it has that kind of clinically unimaginative frontage. I had long since learned, however, that this was the Memorial Hall, headquarters of Lambourn Parish Council, and on this chill February night it was to stage a potentially stormy meeting of the planning sub-committee.

Lambourn may have changed much, expanding considerably in the past twenty years, but the mere mention of developing the self-contained hamlet known as Upper Lambourn touches the most sensitive nerve of the long-standing inhabitants. Somehow, one such suggestion had been given the nod by Newbury District Council, even after being slung out at parish level. The local councillors were stung, outraged even, and the chairman of the western planning committee had agreed to come before them this evening to hear their case. Poor fellow.

Once inside, the hall resembles a college refectory in shape and layout. The walls are painted blue and a portrait of the Queen – that one you see in every council chamber or government office – hangs next to the clock at the business end of the room. A large table had been prepared, surrounded by fifteen chairs, each with a glass stationed in front of it, and a decanter of water stood at the head of the table.

One councillor, a burly man by the name of Charles Oliver-Bellasis, announced his arrival by knocking his glass on to the floor; another, the immaculate Jim Cramsie, glided in sporting a red-and-white handkerchief in his breast pocket and unsmilingly took his place to the right of Chairman Ted Brind. He looked as if he meant business.

There were three rows of public seats at the back of the hall, overlooked by a notice advertising the night's meeting. 'All parishioners are invited to attend' it proclaimed. But none of them had. My only companion was an attractive blonde in a tartan skirt and spectacles. She took hectic shorthand and turned out to be the reporter for the Newbury weekly newspaper.

Ted Brind, having removed his customary sailor's cap, called the meeting to order and invited any relevant questions for the guest, the Hon. Gerald Vane, an architect with a grey moustache and receding hair who spoke with a gently patronizing air and smiled disarmingly as if he had no idea of the heated emotions he was about to tackle.

It began politely. Doug Spragg, flourishing a cigarette-holder and an earnest expression, opened up with a query about greyhound kennels sited in his own area of Lambourn Woodlands. He was concerned about road safety, and also about the noise factor – a phrase with which he must have been relatively familiar, being a Heathrow air traffic controller.

Mr Oliver-Bellasis made a point next. He lives in the hamlet of Eastbury and works as a chartered surveyor; his family are landowners in Hampshire and his ancestors apparently fought against Cromwell. The air of monied distinction hung around him despite a homespun cardigan.

Battle was not seriously joined, however, until Mr Cramsie, sounding like one of the more civilized MPs one can hear amid the pantomime baying of parliament proceedings, launched into a long-winded three-point query regarding a property in Upper Lambourn named Cruck Cottage. This, I had been warned, was the subject which would ignite the meeting, and it did not disappoint. The reporter next to me scribbled ever more furiously as the Hon. Gerald tried his smile again, failed, and then set about his defensive policies with as much dignity as he could muster.

John Nugent, sheriff of Berkshire and a member of the family who had been so influential in Lambourn affairs down the years, had thus far sat quietly at the end of a row. But he volunteered an entrance on to this subject in his capacity as one of the two representatives for the Upper Lambourn district. He was third into bat, raising a finger unostentatiously to attract the chairman's attention and then speaking, slowly and somnolently at first but in steadily raised tones on a subject that he clearly felt very dearly.

It was at this point that the door at the rear of the hall creaked open and Captain Richard Head tiptoed in. Wearing a check jacket and muddy shoes, he crossed the floor to take his seat at the council table. He was over half an hour late and I took it that something had been amiss in his yard. Perhaps Border Incident, his notoriously injury-prone Gold Cup horse, had suffered another set-back? But as the Captain took out his glasses and muttered an apology, Chairman Brind employed some Berkshire bluntness in revealing the truth. Turning to the Hon. Gerald, he introduced Captain Head and explained: 'He is one of the people who have been making that noise outside.' All was explained. Horses apart, Richard's greatest love was bell-ringing, and nothing should keep him from practice night.

The debate on Cruck Cottage and the development which, I understood, had already been commenced, raged on for some time more. Feelings ran high but frustration was as far as it could go. Finally, Ted Brind excused the honourable visitor from any further inquisition. Mr Vane thanked the assembly for their patience, which he might not have noticed wearing distinctly thin, and with a little more of the disarming style, abandoned ship.

There followed a shuffling of feet and papers, a few glances at the kitchen-style clock and the cinema-style exit sign and an eventual resignation to the more menial business still to be discussed. The clerk, Gillian Jenkins, read swiftly through the planning applications to be considered, almost all of which concerned loose boxes or additional accommodation for stable-lads or other racing staff. This, I felt, was more like the Lambourn we all know, even if less exciting than the beration of the Hon. Gerald Vane.

The anti-racing element on the council had their say on a couple of such applications, a lady in a cream anorak making out the major case for the prosecution. But there was never much doubt that permission would be granted, and the reporter, I noticed, was so confident that she had taken to doodling on her agenda paper, checking her diary and doing a formidably lengthy shopping list. At three minutes to nine, when the council moved on to point eight of the agenda, she packed her bag and left me in solitary confinement in the three rows, and I took it that the entertainment was about to close. On the stroke of nine, Chairman Brind wound things up and the councillors scattered. As in most such gatherings, the talking had mainly been done by a few. Three, in fact, had said nothing throughout the meeting.

Richard Head, having been last to arrive, was also last to leave, and as we ventured into the chill night once again, I asked him about Border Incident. His eyes lit up and a smile crossed his face. 'Very well indeed,' he said. 'Ascot next week, and I think he should win.' With that he went back to his house in Upper Lambourn, virtually opposite the cottage development which had been the star of the evening.

It was Snowy Outen, head lad to Barry Hills, who had introduced me to Ted Brind. One early winter morning at the palatial Southbank yard, this splendid village old-timer had said: 'I know just the man for you to see.' And with that, he and his dog had jumped into my car and we had set off to a part of the village new to me. A knock at the front and back door brought no response, but then we saw him, sailor's cap and warm coat intact, strolling up the road from the library where his wife works.

Ted took me into his neat terraced house and, within minutes, I knew that Snowy's judgement was sound. A couple of colour prints of old Lambourn stood on the mantelpiece, and a history of the village lingered in Ted's brain. He had been a union officer by profession but an historian by habit and, since his retirement, filled his days researching the history of Lambourn and its surrounds.

He was waiting for me when I called again at his home, the morning after the planning meeting. Gillian Jenkins was there, too, friendly and efficient, and we sat at Ted's dining table and talked. I learned that Ted had been born 'over the border' in Wiltshire, but had come to live in Lambourn at eleven and stayed until he went out to work six years later.

'I joined the Post Office at Newbury as an apprentice. One way and another, I stayed with them all my working life, ending up as an officer in the legal department of the Post Office Engineering Union.'

Ted did not appear to meet the requirements of militancy or clichéd jargon which so many unions seem to demand these days. 'I always used to be fond of researching history,' he explained. 'My spare time was spent in libraries, and when I came back to Lambourn in 1975, I began looking into the background of the place by going through old books at Reading Library. Whenever my wife wanted to go shopping, we would go to Reading, and I disappeared into the reference library. She always knew where to find me.'

Ted was sixty-three, and probably knew more about Lambourn than anyone with the exception of John Penfold, who had been clerk to the council for much of his life and lived just opposite John Rodbourn on Hungerford Hill. But Mr Penfold was intent on keeping his knowledge to himself. Mr Brind was much more helpful.

He produced an old ledger, impeccably kept, in which the minutes of every council meeting from its inception in 1894 up to 1927 were recorded. The writing was remarkably clear, but business appeared to have been brief in those days. 'The parish council was set up following a public meeting in the schoolroom, which was then opposite the post office, on 4 December 1894,' he related. 'On the thirteenth of the same month they had a meeting.' He pointed to the entry, and one name at least was familiar. There was a Penfold on the council even then. 'It seems that meetings seldom lasted longer than fifteen minutes in the early years. The main reason is that there were no planning applications to consider.'

He produced another ledger, slightly later in vintage. 'Read through these two,' he said, 'and in a matter of minutes you are through the Boer War, the Great War and the Second World War, virtually without knowing anyone was fighting. The only reference I have found in that respect is a dance that was held in the Memorial Hall in

1940, which is stated to have been in aid of China.'

The other odd thing about the minutes, which had not eluded Ted either, was that they chose to ignore racing almost entirely, even though it was a major and growing industry in the village.

There was plenty else to stimulate the imagination, however, like details of the pest house in Baydon Road for those considered unclean. It was apparently built with public subscription and, when public sensitivity increased, changed its name to an Isolation Hospital. It continued in that guise into the 1930s, but is now a private house.

But Ted's information was not confined to minute-reading. He told me all about the Isbury Almshouses, which stand to the north of the church, and their colourful history. Their founder was John Estbury, in 1501, and legend has it that the almsmen were obliged to pray daily for his soul. He died in 1507 and local historians will tell you he was killed when a worm dropped into his mouth as he lay sleeping. His housekeeper tried to remove the worm by tipping a basin of hot milk into his mouth after it, apparently, and the eventual cause of death was a stung lip . . .

Ted sat at his table thinking back to his childhood years in Lambourn. 'It has changed so much since then,' he said. 'When I was young, Ossie Bell was the biggest trainer in the village, and he never had more than sixty horses in. There are several with many more than that now.'

Ted is not a racing man himself and, although he has a regular beer in the local pubs, mixes with the lads and takes an interest in the fortunes of the yards and their horses, he concerns himself chiefly with mediating on the council between those involved in the sport and those who feel they should oppose its development. 'We recognize the conflict and do all we can to resolve it. For some years, there has been a move to shift the racing stables out of the centre of the village. Not many of the major trainers are on the main streets now, but we do have to deal with people who are, frankly, frightened by the strings from Barry Hills, Nick Henderson and others coming down the main streets. The yearlings, those who have never been on a racecourse and are still frisky and not fully trained, tend to jump all over the place when they are walking, and elderly people on the pavements do get scared. Horse paths should have been constructed years ago,' he conceded. 'But somehow there was a slip-up and it has remained an issue up to now.'

Like most others who have spent more than a few months in the village, Ted's sympathy for the newcomers who arrive, treating Lambourn as just another dormitory for London, and then instantly launch complaints about the horse industry which has been there for generations, is strictly limited. They are entitled to a voice, but it may not be heeded.

Gillian Jenkins has lived in Lambourn all her life and, although far from being a regular race-goer, understands the conflict better than most. She lives in a recently-constructed cul-de-sac, opposite the British Legion, wherein have settled a number of jockeys and lads, together with some newcomers. Gillian has observed the relationship and the problems but knows there is no miracle cure.

Her chairman, naturally enough, prefers to reflect quietly on generations past, such as the men from Lambourn who took part in the agricultural riots of the 1830s and were deported for their misdemeanors. 'There was a well-known incident on Easby Bridge, just outside the village,' he says. 'Three men were standing there, one of them with a stick, and the local blacksmith reported the fact to the police, before times were so sensitive. The sergeant arrived and arrested all three for a riotous assembly. They apparently all worked for a local farmer and were debating ways to back up their claim for two shillings a week extra. I don't know what happened to the other two, but the man with the stick was shipped to Australia.'

The Nugent family has a ubiquitous influence over Lambourn life. They are talked of like village squires, a distinction to which they would not lay claim, for if the village remains faintly feudal, there is no suggestion that the best-known landowners and employers are anything but good news for the community.

Brothers David and John perpetuate a family tradition in Lambourn stretching back three generations to their great grandfather Sir Charles Nugent, who came to train racehorses in the village in the latter years of the last century. After using a number of other bases, he finally settled at Windsor House. John paraphrases the distant family history with a crisp clarity. 'Sir Charles's son, our grandfather, was killed riding in 1904. Sir Charles himself lived until 1927 and by that time had brought over our father, Sir Hugh Nugent, to continue training at Windsor House.'

As ever, the path to family prosperity and distinction was not without its unpleasant pitfalls. Sir Charles had become a heavy drinker. He also gambled recklessly. The combination was disastrous. John relates: 'He had virtually drunk and gambled away everything the family had. My father had to sell up the furniture to pay his way when he took on Windsor House.'

Sir Hugh Nugent married in 1931 and within four years, the two boys were born. Other than horses, Sir Hugh's trade was as a motor mechanic, and in 1930, the garage in Lambourn High Street was opened, which John Nugent runs to this day. At first it operated on a small scale, a man named Frank Thatcher supervising the workshop while Sir Hugh concentrated on his training business, just up the road. But the seeds of enterprise were quickly sown; Frank and Sir Hugh decided they should go into a horse transport business together, and started it by purchasing a box from another company.

From these exploratory beginnings swelled the conglomerate which became known as Lambourn Holdings and, until the recent sale of two Newbury garages and an engineering company, employed more than five hundred people.

Sir Hugh took his family back to their ancestral land, Ireland, in 1938, and there he stayed. Windsor House had apparently been a rather weighty handicap since the exploits of Sir Charles, so the disused family house in Ireland had been patched up as a base once more. Sir Hugh continued his work in the motor business and enhanced his reputation as an innovator. One of his achievements was to bring hydro-electric power to his native village.

The Lambourn garage was still run as a family business and administered by Frank Thatcher during the war years, while Sir Hugh served in the air force. In 1959, John Nugent, the elder of the two brothers by a couple of years, returned to the village with his new wife Pepe.

'I think I had always wanted to come back, chiefly because the garage was there. I loved cars in those days – more than I do after twenty-odd years in the trade, I have to admit – and I had learned the business during four years at Rootes in Coventry. I ended up as assistant to the managing director, Sir Geoffrey Rootes, before deciding the time was right to branch out and run my own organization. Lambourn was pre-ordained as the place to do it.

'At the time of moving back, I remembered very little of my childhood days in the village, but over the course of time things happened to jog my memory. Certainly, I grew to love the place and to involve myself in the life of the village.'

With his grey hair, large round glasses and studious gaze, John Nugent has the air of a prep-school headmaster. But he is essentially a doer, not a talker, and in the past two decades he has expanded the garage and horse transport business in the village at a quite startling rate. His most ambitious venture, however, was doomed by industrial troubles. A factory, large and impressively equipped, was built in the neighbouring village of Membury as the base for the Lambourn Cab company. It failed due to three separate strikes at crucial stages of its establishment, and John Nugent wisely sold off his interest in the development. Late in 1981, it was announced that the factory would close, with the loss of more than 160 jobs. The horse box business and its day-to-day running is left chiefly in the capable hands of Jim Cramsie. The garage, John directs himself with great elan.

Brother David, meanwhile, is the largest landowner in the area. He was given Limes Farm, a vast area including the most used of the downs gallops, by his father, and apart from supervising his property, he also trains race-horses under a permit.

It is here that John deviates from the family line, for despite his deep involvement in Lambourn life he has no great interest in racing. The reason, he suggests, is a direct throwback to the sorrowful demise of great-grandfather Sir Charles. 'He had so much at one time. He had won the Grand National and he had a marvellous house. But when his son was killed on a racecourse his life seemed to change. I did not want to go that way, and perhaps subconsciously I avoided all possibility. I once owned two horses, it is true. But that was a fleeting involvement and although I am inevitably involved in the perimeter of the sport through living and working with so many in the business, it has never really attracted me.'

At the parish council meeting I attended on that bleak February night, John Nugent made his impression in the restrained, gentlemanly but firm fashion which, I would guess, has distinguished him throughout his fifteen years of service on that body, two of them as chairman. It may be fashionable, even traditional, for people to despise their employers, but I could not imagine too many people having bitter words for John.

9·Dreams Die at Cheltenham

OLIVER Sherwood sat in the front room of his cosy eighteenth-century cottage, his month-old dog nibbling at his fingers as he reflected on Cheltenham just as a small boy might reflect on Christmas. 'For months beforehand, everything we do is geared to the meeting,' he said. 'We all talk about it and look forward to it, and Lambourn virtually stands still for it. Then, quite suddenly, it has gone. The night after the Gold Cup feels such an anti-climax.'

For Sherwood it had been more of a let-down than usual this year. Those months of preparation can never have been so full of hope and excitement as his father's horse Venture to Cognac was nursed back to fitness and aimed with real optimism at the Gold Cup. But on the day of reckoning he had been found wanting, along with most of the other fancied runners. The Sherwoods were left to drown their sorrows and think vaguely of next year.

Cruel setback it may sound, but Lambourn is full of them. Every day of every week, whether the racing is at Cheltenham or Newton Abbott, Ascot or Yarmouth, hopes and dreams are dismantled and destroyed. The difference is, if it happens at Cheltenham the sufferer merits more sympathy. Not that Sherwood would be grateful for sympathy. Bred into his system is the dogma of all racing folk – yesterday is forgotten, today is almost over, but tomorrow is another chance of winning. It is this very phlegmatic philosophy which keeps stable-lads smiling when many others in their financial position would weep. It gives trainers faith during lean times and jockeys new heart when three successive fancied runners have fallen.

Sherwood did not come from such a background. Nat, his father, farms in Essex and his racing involvement had always been confined to point-to-point courses. He had ridden more than sixty winners in that sphere and now, in comfortable later life, owns the course at Marks Tey, near Colchester. But the most important ingredient in racing, the horses, were always around and Oliver grew up with some kind of equine life his main ambition. He went to public school at Radley and confesses to being 'academically hopeless'. He had no desire to go on to university and, not being under any parental pressure to plunge into a business career, spent his first year of freedom in Australia.

'When I came back I worked for my father at first, and then joined Gavin Pritchard-Gordon's stable in Newmarket. I had not been there long when a job came up in Ireland as head lad to Arthur Moore in County Kildare.' Sherwood took that job and neither he nor Moore ever regretted it. Their working association lasted three years, in which Oliver virtually acted as assistant trainer, and they have remained close friends ever since. They are linked not just by a public school education – Moore went to Downside – and a love of racing, but by one particular horse. For it was at Moore's yard, on the edge of the Kildare peat bogs, that Venture to Cognac began his career.

Lambourn's great Gold Cup hope had fetched only £950 when sold at the Doncaster sales as a three-year-old and Moore, a young but ambitious trainer, took him to Ireland and ran him in some bumper events, flat races for National Hunt horses. Within six months he was sold again – to Nat Sherwood, who wanted a horse on which Oliver could start point-to-point riding. 'I was sorry to lose him,' relates Arthur Moore now, 'but in truth none of us had any idea what a horse he would turn out to be.'

Oliver himself certainly hadn't, but when he returned to England to replace Nicky Henderson as assistant to

Fred Winter, the horse came with him. 'I would not have left Ireland for any other job,' he says. 'But Nicky was getting married and setting up his own yard, and I also had the chance to buy his cottage in Eastbury. All in all, it looked too good a package to refuse. I had never even set foot in Lambourn, and Fred Winter was simply a god to me. I had not met him before, but I knew plenty about him. Funnily enough, the first thing he asked me when we met was whether I had a decent horse to ride. I mentioned Cognac, hoping he would be good enough!' Sherwood and Winter struck up a good relationship immediately; for Oliver, the move was to have delightful side-benefits as he is now marred to Fred's daughter, Denise, and they still live in the converted eighteenth-century vicarage he bought from Nicky Henderson.

For Venture to Cognac, the move to Lambourn was also a great success. 'Half-way through his five-year-old career we began to realize his potential,' says Oliver. 'Then he won a good race at Newbury by twenty-five lengths and I knew he would be top class.' Sherwood's only early reservation about his horse was its odd name. 'When you register a horse for racing, you have to list five choices of names. We thought of four that we liked; this was a last resort, but it was the one we were given. At first, I couldn't stand it, but I suppose it grew on me as he started to win races!'

But, as so often happens in steeplechasing, injury blighted the progress of a potential star. Just as Venture to Cognac seemed ready to fulfil all his promise, leg trouble of the worst type set him back. For long periods, it seemed likely that he would never be fit enough to run in a Gold Cup, let alone win one. The Sherwoods did not despair, however, and through the regular and devoted attentions of Lambourn vet Spike Kirby, Cognac returned to racing early in the 1981–2 season, the Gold Cup in view.

The treatment given to the horse was based on a substance made from the juice of cocks' combs. It may smack of a gypsy's potion, but it worked, restoring Cognac to race fitness despite occasional spells of lameness. One such alarm occurred two weeks before Cheltenham and news of it was never allowed to escape from the Winter stables.

'He went lame on a Saturday morning,' recalls Oliver, 'and we decided to keep it quiet and hope. By Monday morning he was perfectly alright again. Nobody knows why or how it happened, we were just relieved that the panic was past.'

So, in sunshine, high winds and the occasional authentic springtime squall, Lambourn's jumping season reached its annual high with the three-day Festival, a very special meeting which rivets even those whose business or pleasure is usually concentrated on the more clinical flat-racing circuit.

Lambourn's training tribe advanced on the big week with mixed feelings. The Winter horses were being irritatingly inconsistent, and several other local trainers – Nicky Henderson among them – had disappointed their own high expectations. But at Nick Gaselee's yard, the indomitable David Mooney led up the eighteenth winner of his brief life as a lad and taffy Byron Mills sat over his pint of lager in The George that night shaking a toothy grin and wondering good-naturedly 'how the lucky bastard does it'.

Harry Foster missed a night in the cocktail bar at The Red Lion and Flo, Marje and the rest of the regulars fretted for his safety. And then, Lambourn life was disturbed by a real tragedy as John Thorne, one of the nicest men anyone could have hoped to know, fell from one of his own horses at a point-to-point meeting and was killed. He wasn't a Lambourn man but that didn't matter a damn. The village mourned for Nicky's father-in-law, a man who had epitomized the fortitude that racing demanded and received from so many.

Life had to go on. Cheltenham approached rapidly, and

last-minute preparations were as hectic as ever. Tempers shortened, worries lengthened and butterflies found their way into the stomachs of even the most hardened jockeys and trainers. It happens every March.

Venture to Cognac's schedule had been met. His final race before the Gold Cup was a triumph, giving weight and a severe beating to Dramatist, a result even more popular at the Winter headquarters because the opposition came from the Walwyns, 'over the wall'. All that was left was the daily routine of work to maintain and sharpen fitness, and this was always in the hands of Oliver and the horse's lad, Pete Maddison. 'He did a couple of pieces of serious work each week, and spent other days walking around the all-weather track at Nicky Henderson's yard. He won't trot on the roads like most horses. He doesn't like it at all, and we are not going to force him.'

For days before the festival, rain fell relentlessly from dark skies over the Cotswolds. It did not concern the Sherwoods, safe in the belief that their horse would operate on heavy going; but it worried the staff at Cheltenham, and on the eve of the opening they confessed that the first day would have to be abandoned unless there was a swift change of weather. Divine intervention may have nothing to do with it, but it did seem a coincidence that the Clerk of the Course, Major Philip Arkwright, had scarcely uttered these gloomy words when the clouds began to break, the rain ceased and a decent wind sprang up to begin drying the floods. At dawn the following morning, the stewards decided that racing could go ahead.

Perhaps the god of weather is an Irishman. It certainly seemed a probability when the Irish mopped up the first three races on the opening day's card, notably the Champion Hurdle in which For Auction caused a sensation at 40–1. Fred Winter's Derring Rose was one of Lambourn's hopefuls in this event, and on the night before the race John Francome was eating in The Five

Bells at Wickham when he noticed a hunting horn on the
bar. Knowing that Derring Rose was a difficult sort who
had apparently been sweetened by hunting, he borrowed
the horn, jokingly promising to blow it at the start of the
race. The story has no happy postscript. Derring Rose,
despite all Francome's efforts, pulled himself up and was
promptly retired from the racetrack.

By Wednesday evening, hours before the Gold Cup,
Cheltenham's new betting and boozing facilities had been
fully tested by two crowds in excess of twenty thousand.
Litter was strewn across the walkways as boys purveying
three different evening newspapers wandered from bar to
bar announcing their goods; I wondered how on earth the
staff would spruce the place up for the following day, and
didn't envy them their job.

Night Nurse was a warm favourite for the race,
followed in the betting by Royal Bond and Venture to
Cognac. Another coincidence here, as Royal Bond is
trained by Arthur Moore and had been ridden in his first
two races in Ireland by Oliver Sherwood. Moore smiled
slowly at the memory. 'I have spoken to Oliver on the
phone several times in the past few weeks,' he said. 'We
have compared notes, without giving anything away. But
I'm not prepared to say which I think is the better horse
until the race is over.'

In Lambourn that night there were more suits, ties and
tips than usual. Almost everyone in the village pubs had
either been to Cheltenham or watched the races on
television; without exception, they had firm opinions on
the outcome of the race tomorrow, but few views
coincided. In The George, landlady Maureen and barmaid Ruby wanted Night Nurse to win, chiefly for
sentimental reasons. In the Catholic Club, where a large
gathering of Irishmen were celebrating St Patrick's Day in
some style, Royal Bond was the natural choice. But
Lambourn's heavy money had gone on Venture to
Cognac. Dottie at The Five Bells confirmed that most of

her customers had backed the horse; Jimmy Gold in The Red Lion confessed that he had invested a sizeable sum himself, and that in his pub that night there were a good deal of racing lads with a tidy proportion of their month's wages resting on the performance of Cognac.

Oliver Sherwood suspected as much but, fortunately for his own peace of mind, did not know the worst. 'I was glad that the lads in the yard didn't niggle at me about the horse,' he explained. 'I would have worried if I had known they'd had a lot of money on it.'

I breakfasted at The George next morning. On the next table was a trio of Irishmen, over for the meeting. They had been present at the Catholic Club the previous night; when that wound up, they had played dominoes back at the pub. They confessed to having enjoyed themselves with a few drinks, but were studying their copies of the *Sporting Life* with surprisingly bright eyes.

Ten o'clock at Uplands found the Winter horsebox in position. Navy blue, with a cream sash, it stood in the yard with its ramp down waiting for the day's runners to board, Venture to Cognac among them. At the back of the yard, a group of lads were doing the ritual sweeping-up and peering suspiciously at my presence, protective about their charges on such an important day.

The roads and fields of Upper Lambourn were all still flooded, a sure indication that the going had barely improved. Outside Nick Gaselee's cottage a black limousine was being washed; a little further down the lane Richard Head and his wife Alicia prepared to leave for the course to watch their beloved Border Incident attempt the Gold Cup. Like Venture to Cognac, he had suffered lengthily from injuries, and despite the beaming confidence of his trainer, the bookies still offered 40–1. They found few takers, even in Lambourn.

At Saxon House the grand old man of the game, Fulke Walwyn, was seeing off his Gold Cup hope Diamond Edge. Consistently unlucky in the race, Walwyn's star was now faced by the type of sticky conditions he loathed most; but the sociable band of Walwyn lads had been hopeful in The Maltshovel last night, and would doubtless be glued to a television that afternoon.

The stable-lads' behaviour altered in Cheltenham week, if only slightly. They still went for a pint or two at lunchtime, and still gravitated from the pub to the betting shop. But by first-race time they were home, the television on and their money invested. Sue Hawkins, manager of the betting shop, reported an afternoon spent virtually alone on Thursday 18 March.

I drove to Cheltenham via Winchcombe, the village which lies just over the brow of Cleeve Hill, five miles from Prestbury Park. It was a forest of *Sporting Lifes* and furrowed brows; the pubs filled rapidly with well-dressed businessmen intent on a profitable day off, and tweed-suited farmers on their annual pilgrimage. For me it was a swift pint of beer before diving back on to the switchback road to the course, now a cluttered convoy of race-goers. I made good time until the police stopped all the traffic for no apparent reason; it transpired that the Queen Mother, having picked up her mints from the Cheltenham sweet shop she patronizes each year, was now being escorted on the final leg of her journey to the course.

At about the time that I was sitting in the queue, Oliver Sherwood was sipping a glass of champagne at the house of his friend and fellow amateur rider, Jim Wilson. This was no dereliction of duty, more a loyalty to traditional habits. Also, I suspect, an aid to the troublesome nerves. 'Jim only lives a few minutes from the course, and each year he has lunch parties before racing,' said Sherwood. 'I allowed myself one glass of bubbly and a little to eat. The company is settling, but to be honest I was a lot less nervous than I had been a few days earlier. It had already been a hectic week, which had helped. I had only one ride on each of the earlier days, but for the first I had needed to lose six or seven pounds – I ate out, and ate properly, that night! Denise and I were out to dinner each evening, and I was still getting up at the usual time to ride first lot and go through my regular jobs. Nothing changes, just for Cheltenham.

'My father had arrived to stay with us for the meeting, and was far more tense about the whole thing than I was. But I know he was revelling in the occasion, loving the thrill of actually having a runner in the Gold Cup. Most of my family were due at the race, other than my young brother who was taking exams that day – and I think it helped to have them there and know that I was really riding for them rather than somebody else.'

Sherwood arrived at the course an hour before racing began. The crowd was already enormous, growing to a peak of around fifty thousand. Picnics continued in the car parks, the bars were popular with hair-of-the-dog devotees, public telephones were full and queues stretched outside with punters waiting anxiously to invest. The air was charged with expectancy, and it was dry, breezy air. The weather gods were still smiling, and a springlike sun was throwing shadows across the course. It was bright and clear, and I mused that the inhabitants of the houses set high up on Cleeve Hill would today have a fine view of the race without leaving their gardens.

The Gold Cup was the third race on the card, and when the jockeys came out to the new parade ring, a huge crowd was banked around the terraces looking down on the scene. Sherwood took his instructions from Fred Winter, shared a last word and glance with his father, then swung himself on board. 'The guv'nor did not try to confuse me with too many orders. He never does. All he said was to keep to the inside as much as possible. The rest he left up to me.'

But one very significant piece of advice had already been passed on by Jim Wilson, who rode the victorious Little Owl in the race twelve months earlier and would have partnered him again but for a mysterious injury to the horse. Sherwood recalls: 'Jim told me I must be six lengths closer to the leaders than I wanted to be, because the race was always run very fast. He was absolutely right. They all set off as if it was a two-mile race, rather than three and a half. And several of us were never really going well.'

The three best-backed horses in the field, Night Nurse, Royal Bond and Venture to Cognac, never troubled the leaders, the favourite actually being pulled up on the second circuit. Sherwood feared something similar: 'As we went past the stands and set out on the final circuit, I thought I might have to pull him up,' he admits. 'To his great credit, he kept going, but he lacked the sparkle I had come to expect from him, and we were never going to get near the winner.'

Silver Buck won it for the northern stable of Michael Dickinson, who also trained the second-placed Bregawn. Venture to Cognac was seventh, and Sherwood quietly walked him back to the unsaddling area for also-rans, while the crowd acclaimed the winner in the amphitheatre of the new enclosure. Silver Buck delightedly kicked his hind legs as Robert Earnshaw – unknown a few months earlier – jumped down, and Dickinson hurried from one to the other of his horses like a clucking mother hen.

The losing jockeys trailed round the back way to the weighing-room like the footballers who have just lost the cup final. And back in Lambourn, as Richard Pitman began his review of the race on television, a hundred and one stable-lads ruefully counted their losses. Knowing them, it would have been only a matter of minutes before the perkiness returned and conversation turned to the next race on the card.

Oliver Sherwood did not have another ride that day. He returned to Frisky's Place, his Eastbury cottage, and flopped into an armchair. 'I felt completely exhausted. Also, I suppose, deflated. I had thought about the race so much beforehand, and now it was over. We hadn't won, and although I did not like to think of it as a failure, we had no real excuse for defeat. I ate a steak and watched television, turning on the video to see the race again. Once more, I was surprised at the pace of the race. Jim had been right. But in the end, even his advice had made no difference.

'The rest of the season seemed to stretch out ahead with no real incentives. An anti-climax. There was Liverpool to come in a fortnight, and I still hoped Rolls Rambler would run to give me my first ride in the Grand National – that was a real ambition. But after that, nothing. I tend to become a little lazy in the last few weeks of a season, not bothering to waste for rides. But there is always next year to look forward to. I shall go away to Spain in the summer, to get right away from horses for a few weeks. Then I shall play some cricket, and go to Lord's a few times, so I come back to the job really refreshed.'

Oliver was twenty-seven a week after the Gold Cup. He had plenty of time left, both as jockey and, in all probability, trainer. Fulke Walwyn had less time. True, he had already won the race four times as a trainer, but Diamond Edge continued to fall just short of his highest hopes. This year, running gallantly in the mud he hates, he was fourth. Similar frustrations had beset Richard Head. He knew he may never have a better horse than Border Incident. But, clearly out of sorts once again, he had been pulled up by John Francome.

Lambourn's Cheltenham had not been a wild success story, for trainers, jockeys or the punting stable-lads. But as the village returned to normal, they were all already talking of next year.

10·The Aintree Adventure

THE final week of March is the busiest time of year in Lambourn. While all those involved in jump racing count their bruises after Cheltenham and gird their loins for the marvellous, eccentrically British marathon at Aintree, the flat racing machine starts up.

It is not only the stable staff and secretaries who are now flat out; from Frank Mahon and his fellow vets to Tony Halestone at his forge, all the people employed in racing's peripheral trades and professions find their diaries filling up fast. At the transport depot, Jim Cramsie and his staff are long past the idle, anxious times of midwinter; the drivers' rest room is virtually empty now. And at E. J. Wicks' saddlery establishment, 'Blood' Bentick and his assistants are working long into the night to meet demand. But if the advent of the commercial, stud-orientated half of the sport causes an immediate flutter of excitement around the village, its rule is brief. Within a week, people are talking once more of jumping, and of only one race.

The last time a Lambourn horse won the Grand National was in 1966, when Fred Winter's Anglo ridden by Tim Norman was the fourth successive winner to come out of the village. It was a long time to wait for another celebration with beer and bunting in the square, and the 1982 field gave some cause for optimism that the waiting might be over. Of the thirty-nine horses which lined up at the start just before 3.20 p.m. on 3 April, nine were trained in Lambourn. There might have been more, but the final few days before the toughest race of all provided a saga of misfortunes. The old adage that it is harder to get a horse and jockey to the race fit than it is to win it, seemed unhappily appropriate.

Richard Head was no different from anyone else in his dreams of training the National winner, except that since 1980 he had been widely expected to do so. It was then, in the Topham Trophy race which is run two days before the National over one circuit of the fearsome course, that Head's eleven-year-old Uncle Bing gave such an inspired display of jumping in his victory under John Francome that it had seemed only a matter of time before he graduated to the real thing and made his trainer a happy man.

Steeplechasing in general, and the Grand National in particular, is very seldom as predictable as that, however. Training problems prevented 'Bingo', as the horse is known at his Upper Lambourn home, from running in the 1981 race, but this year he had been prepared with only the National in mind. Richard was patently excited at the prospect especially as his other stable star, Border Incident, seemed unable to free himself satisfactorily from the injuries which had scarred his promising career.

Habitually well-scrubbed, his hair swept back in a military style, Richard looks the part of the village squire. He is not, of course, but the subject arose just before his birthday at the end of February; his manner is indecisive, even elusive, but his tone is friendly. 'Lambourn is not like the ordinary, old-fashioned impression of a village,' he suggested. 'The squire and peasant syndrome has never really applied here. Not even the Nugents could claim to be the squires, for all their influence.' For the past year, Richard had served on the parish council: 'They wanted me as a racing representative, I think, because there is certainly an anti-horse element on the council.' But this was the closest he had come, or was likely to get, to the political peaks achieved by his father. Having ended the war as a Brigadier, he became an MP in 1945 and later Minister of Defence during the Suez crisis. He was also, at various times, High Commissioner for Nigeria and Malaya. 'There was never any pressure applied on me to go into politics,' Richard said, 'and frankly I had neither the mind nor the inclination for it.'

He also had no inclination, in his youth, to venture into the racing world, despite the fact that he lived a stone's throw from Ascot racecourse and that his father had found time amid his many other duties to ride in point-to-point and amateur races. That Richard found his way into the horse world at all was something of a fluke, which it still amuses him to relate now. 'When I joined the army, I was at first in the armoured car regiment of the Life Guards. But then I was posted to the Household Cavalry, and on my first day at Knightsbridge Barracks, I realized what I had been missing. The involvement with horses was mandatory, of course, and I had not really been looking forward to it. The other chaps in the regiment had always read the *Sporting Life* over breakfast and I had never shown the slightest interest. But once I started to live and work among horses, I knew that this was for me. I started hunting regularly, and when a six-month equitation course at Melton Mowbray transpired, involving two days of hunting each week, I applied for it like a shot, and was accepted.

'Soon, I wanted a horse of my own to hunt. I worked a good dodge here. I knew that if I could find a perfectly black horse of sixteen hands, I could call it my officer's charger, and its keep would be paid. Purely by chance I found the ideal animal. He was called Beau Caprice and owned by Lady Arran. I paid £250 and it turned out to be more of a bargain than I had imagined. After a few months of hunting, I thought I would enter a point-to-point. We won without any trouble at all, but the horse then fell four times in succession. Some friends suggested that I should try running him under Rules, over hurdles, and I agreed it was worth a try. My interest was ripening now, and I sent Beau Caprice to Fulke Walwyn, then the champion trainer. His yard was pretty full, of course, but he agreed to look at the horse for a month and let me know. When the time came, Fulke said, "He's alright, I'll train him." I was later to learn just how high a tribute that was, coming from him. Beau Caprice was then thirteen, a remarkable age to be starting out on a novice hurdles career. But he won two minor races at Wincanton and then romped up in the Gloucester Hurdle at Cheltenham. By now I was hooked. I had decided that my future lay in training racehorses.'

By a route which involved working for Peter Cazalet, Alec Head and, ironically, Fulke Walwyn, Richard reached the point when he was ready to set out alone, and secured his present yard in the backwater of Upper Lambourn. 'I bought it from David Nugent, but it was once Reg Hobbs' yard, and he trained winners of the Gold Cup and Grand National here,' Head explained. 'I'm told, though, that it was once owned by the Earl of Craven, who used it as a yard for carthorses – farm animals in the stables, and the carts at the back.'

Richard seems idyllically happy in his domain. His training results have been by no means negligible, but neither has he fulfilled the promise which perennially seems to exist at his yard. Border Incident should have won a Gold Cup, people say, and Uncle Bing should certainly win a National. Now, tragically, neither is possible.

'Bingo's' approach to the race was quiet, maybe too quiet. One pipe-clearing run at Newbury, in which he was ridden by champion-elect Peter Scudamore, filled the camp with optimism. Richard decided he should have only one further outing before Aintree, and penned it in for Wincanton on 11 March. Not surprisingly for a horse with such high ambitions, Uncle Bing was installed as a warm favourite but, ridden by John Francome, struggled into third place, thirty-five lengths adrift of the winner. Francome jumped off and drawled: 'He was terrible, needed the race very badly. It was the worst ground I've ever ridden on over fences, though.' With that winning smile of his to the owners he added, 'He'll be all right.' The stewards took a dim view of the proceedings and fined Head £200 for 'schooling in public'. Captain Head left looking glum, and who could blame him? He had arrived on this blustery Somerset day with every hope of winning the race as a stepping stone to Aintree. He left with the race lost, a hefty hole in his pocket and the ladder to Aintree collapsed under him.

Uncle Bing did not run again. He was schooled and galloped by Bob Champion, the reigning champion jockey of Aintree, seven days before the race at Newbury. By that stage both John Francome and Peter Scudamore had passed up the ride and former champion Jonjo O'Neill had been booked, a highly capable deputy. But during the Newbury gallop, 'Bingo' aggravated an old back injury. With heavy heart, Richard Head decided the horse must be retired.

By the time I saw her in April, Jenny Pitman's tears had long since dried. But hers is still among the most poignant of Grand National stories, if only because her personal disaster followed a number of other unkind twists of fate. It was on the Lambourn gallops, one bleak morning at the back end of January, that Lord Gulliver dropped dead. He had been in Jenny's yard for five years and was considered a prime contender for the National this year. Jenny's sister and stable secretary Mandy was riding Lord Gulliver in his work; Jenny, as usual, was watching from a distance as the horror unfolded.

'I shall never forget the sight, no matter how toughened I may become,' she recalls. 'This was the first horse I had ever bought from Ireland. He was big, black and good-looking – as soft as grease and my personal favourite of them all in the yard. I suppose it always happens to the favourites. . . . He had a heart attack, that was clear. It was as if he was throwing a fit, and it was only lucky he did not carry a couple of other horses into the fence with him as he plunged about. Mandy was thrown off, I saw that much before running to get to them. It was a quarter of a mile to the Land-Rover, and another half-mile to the horses, so it took me a fair while. When I got there, Mandy was sobbing her heart out. My first feeling was one of complete shock. I looked at this beautiful animal lying on the grass and I said: "He looks pretty ordinary down there, doesn't he?"

'Mandy and I both had tears in the Land-Rover, but I pulled myself together and told her not to waste her tears, it was all over. She was so upset, though, that she went home for four days. The hardest part was telling the owners. It always is. Peter Callender owned Lord Gulliver, and he is such a nice bloke I didn't know how to approach it. But he works in the music business, with a lot of success, and fortunately he had been working all night and was still in bed when I summoned the courage to phone. I told his wife, and Peter phoned back later. I still didn't know what to say, and I felt myself starting to cry again . . . but he was very good about it.'

Jenny told me the story while puffing on a cigarette and emotions were only just under control, even at a distance of time. If she had consolation at all, it was in the presence of two further Grand National horses in her yard, Monty Python and Artistic Prince. But Lord Gulliver could never be replaced.

Bad luck would not release Jenny. Weavers Point, her top four-year-old hurdler, ran splendidly in a hot race at Newbury a week before Aintree, but had to be put down immediately afterwards. Mrs Pitman arrived at Liverpool needing a tonic.

Oliver Sherwood made no secret of the fact that his greatest riding ambition was a mount in the National. He was adamant on the point when we talked at Uplands early in the season. At that stage, Venture to Cognac was by no means a certain Gold Cup entry and if anything it seemed more likely that Sherwood's big-race riding would be confined to Aintree, where the hunter-chaser Rolls Rambler was pencilled in as his probable partner. The road to Liverpool, however, was as fraught for them as it was for Richard Head and Jenny Pitman. Rolls Rambler was due to make his seasonal debut in March, but a technical hitch over invalid flu vaccinations proved catastrophic. Despite the protestations of Fred Winter and the gloomy horror of all those in his yard, the horse was effectively ruled out of racing until the Aintree meeting itself. He could run either in the Foxhunters, over the National course, or in the daunting marathon itself. He could even run in both.

A fortnight before the meeting, Oliver had persuaded himself that he would have to wait another year. 'The guv'nor reckons we should go for the Foxhunters and leave the National for this season,' he reported. 'I think he's probably right, too,' was the reluctant admission.

But in the week which followed, views were revised, and as the Aintree programme approached, it was made known that Rambler would go for the National, providing he suffered no ill effects from his outing two days earlier. Oliver Sherwood was about to realize his prime ambition.

It seemed nothing more could go wrong, but on Tuesday, 30 March, two days before Aintree and in his last booked ride before the Foxhunters, Oliver suffered the ultimate disappointment. His mount was Double Bluff in the 5 p.m. race at Kempton, and the partnership was dissolved at the third fence. Oliver fell awkwardly and broke his collarbone, normally no more than an irritating yet accepted interruption for a jockey but, in this of all weeks, cruel in the extreme.

The rides on Rolls Rambler – in both races as it turned out – went to Oliver's great friend Jim Wilson, and while he would have wished his deputy well with genuine sincerity, Oliver could not have been blamed for uttering a few rich curses under his breath as he wandered around the Liverpool course with his arm in a sling, suspended along with his ambition.

For Nick Gaselee, the disappointment was delayed, and certainly different from that of his village compatriots. He had not been among those fretting over the well-being of their National entry, because for some while before the race he had not had one. Keengaddy had been taken out of the race after some disappointing preliminary runs, and was entered instead for the Topham Trophy, run over two and a half miles of the National course on the first day of the meeting. Dave Mooney was there to lead him up, as usual making a great deal of noise and forcing the long-suffering Byron Mills to push his check cap on to the back of his head and pull a face which was half-grin, half-grimace. For David, the arrangement was ideal – it meant he had a trip to Liverpool, with the overnight stop which all lads mean to enjoy despite the relative discomfort of their hostel accommodation, and he could still get back home in time to play football on Saturday. What is more, he was as confident as ever that 'Gadds' would win, and no doubt backed his judgement with somewhat scornful bookies, who allowed the horse to drift to 20–1 in the market.

They were proved right, but only after a titanic battle which would have had any number of the massed layers anxiously fingering their wads of notes, and the boisterous David frantically wondering just where his loyalties lay. For the finish of the Topham was fought out, in epic Aintree fashion, by Gaselee's Keengaddy and another Lambourn horse, Fulke Walwyn's Beacon Time, ridden as ever by Kevin Mooney. Richard Linley had sent Keengaddy in front at the sixth fence, and kept him there until two from home. When Beacon Time, the favourite, took up the running the race looked over, but Linley conjured a thrilling rally from his horse and was beaten only by a length and a half after a contest which had twenty-five thousand people roaring themselves hoarse.

The winners' enclosure was a scrum of Lambourn smiles, and if none was broader than Fulke Walwyn's – for the maestro had never previously won the Topham – Gaselee and Linley were doing their best to mask the nagging let-down of second place with the sheer exhilaration of the run. Linley was still grinning an hour later when we met. He shook his head happily: 'I never knew it could be quite such a thrill riding round that course,' he said. But the next sentence showed how his thoughts ran. 'Maybe he should have run in the National, after all.'

But for Gaselee, Linley, David Mooney and Keengaddy, there was no reversing that decision. They consoled themselves with the knowledge that they had real prospects next year, and settled down to plan the twelve months in between.

Stan Mellor's yard at Mile End, the northernmost tip of Lambourn, housed more National hopes than any other in the country. With just a few days left before the off, the man who rode more National Hunt winners than anyone in history and was awarded the MBE to commemorate it, still had four intended runners in a race he had never won, either as jockey or trainer. Among his entries was Royal Mail, ante-post favourite and the mount of stable jockey Phil Blacker, and Royal Stuart, fourth two years earlier and one of the liveliest outsiders. This, it seemed, could be the year to end Mellor's thirty seasons of trying for that elusive Aintree glory.

I went to Linkslade, the Mellor home, a week before the race. The yard was clean and compact but the man of the house looked more intimidating than his jockey-size stature had any right to permit. He emerged from his office clutching a whip in a manner which suggested menace, and did not put it down throughout our discussion. 'It's just a habit,' he explained at length. 'I don't smoke, and I hardly drink, so I need something to do with my hands.'

Mellor, grey-haired and with deep, penetrating eyes, was proud but not protective of being the only man to ride a thousand jumping winners. 'Someone will beat it one day, I'm sure of that,' he said. 'There are a lot more races now than there were when I was riding, and you must also remember that I was only thirty-five when I stopped, and far from clapped out. I finished because I saw the light, and got to the point where I could see and think about the dangers in jumping. Once that happens, the game is no longer enjoyable and you might as well quit.'

Since starting his second career as a trainer in 1972, Mellor has seen his share of setbacks, but his enjoyment of the job was obvious as he bustled around his yard in front of me, showing off his charges with all the care and detail of the enthusiast as well as the knowledge of the businessman. It was also clear, however, that Stan was restless, searching for new horizons, and that he was about to find them in flat racing.

'Ambitions are limits as much as stimulants,' he said carefully, 'so I don't set specific targets. Good horses and good racing are what interest me, though, and if that means transferring the emphasis of the operation to the flat, I will do it. I thought I might find it a wrench after concentrating on jumping for so much of my life, but in fact it has not turned out that way. I never relished training a large yard of jumpers, for two main reasons. Firstly, I never enjoy August and September or April and May, the bookends of the season, and if the weather cuts into the middle as it so often does, that really doesn't leave much. And secondly, my horses seldom go on heavy ground because I won't have carthorse types here. I like athletic animals, so maybe my inclinations have always been towards the flat. Training two-year-olds is much more fun than training jumpers. You get them as yearlings, so you have first shot at them. By the time they run as two-year-olds, they really seem to be your property, your work. There is no one else to blame if things go wrong. I like it that way.'

It was a sign of the times, and maybe a sad one, that another Lambourn trainer was transferring the bulk of his allegiance to the commercially orientated business of the flat. But, in Mellor's case, the switch would not be immediate or total . . . and first, in any event, there was Liverpool to occupy the mind.

Stan had reservations. 'I would be more fond of Liverpool if it was held in the autumn. I felt the same as a jockey, because with my light weight I was able to pick up a lot of rides and by April I was generally pretty tired and bruised. Now, as a trainer, I feel that the National meeting comes too near the end of the season for horses to be fresh and at their best.'

Most, if not all, of his National quartet, however, had been prepared specifically for the race and Stan gave each one of them a chance of winning. 'Royal Mail's chance is obvious after finishing third last year, but Royal Stuart comes into his own in the spring and is not far behind in my book. Pacify was up beside the leaders when he fell at Becher's on the second circuit last year, and I think Cold Spell is the right type for the race, too. At the moment, we intend to run all four . . . but there is a week left yet.'

Mellor's caution was well-founded. Cold Spell was withdrawn early the following week after going lame at home. That was regrettable enough – certainly for the horse's owner Lord Leverhulme, for whom Mellor had ridden a National second in 1960. But for all at Linkslade, the real drama was yet to come.

There is a better than even chance that the patrons of the Promenade Rest Home, Southport, do not number themselves among the thousands who are captivated by the atmosphere of Aintree. The inhabitants of this worthy establishment are, as the name suggests, there to rest but in National week their peace is disturbed for the Promenade Rest Home has the Royal Clifton Hotel for a neighbour. While this stately, if increasingly seedy, building has the perfectly serene appearance of so much seaside Victoriana, it houses a three-day party each year which even the members of Wodehouse's Drones Club might not survive without the help of a pick-me-up or two.

Those who return each year faithfully disregard the fact that the Liverpool area boasts many better, more comfortable hotels. They are loyal to the Clifton because it is part of their Aintree ritual; without it, the race would not seem the same. The fact that it is sixteen miles from the racecourse does not deter them, nor do the drawbacks of cramped rooms, ancient furniture, soft beds, creaking floors and dilatory service. For in the L-shaped bar nothing changes. The same barmaids, permed, chatty and unconvincingly stern, serve the same drinks to the same people who were there ten years ago – twenty, in some cases. What is more, they will serve them all night, so long as you have one of those cramped rooms to return to and a key to prove it, and so long as you can still stand up and focus on the barmaid to order another. Some, it must be said, pass that stage in the early hours as the nightly party reaches its zenith.

I had stayed at the Clifton for the 1980 race and thought I knew what to expect, but as I passed through the swing doors to check in, after racing on the Thursday, I saw that my fears might be exceeded. Standing at the reception desk with the belligerent expressions of a rugby front-row about to go down for a scrum were, from left to right, John Francome, Philip Blacker and Bill Smith, stable jockeys for Lambourn's three biggest jumping yards, respectively Winter, Mellor and Walwyn. Their common purpose in confronting a harassed clerk was to complain about the standard of accommodation, and more than one uncomplimentary term was heard. The clerk, feverishly fingering his list of bookings, restored order and managed to reallocate rooms, thus at least delaying the jockeys' wrath.

My own room had a sea view, or at least it faced out to sea, which at Southport is rather a different matter. Between the promenade and the lapping waves are an amusement centre, a swimming pool, a park and a pier which stretches away into the distance and defies the pre-breakfast stroller to attempt it. From my window I could also look down past the Rest Home to the alleyways which lead through chip shops, rock stalls and the occasional disco to the town's wide and attractive main street. It was about as far removed from the dust, bustle and cosmopolitan clutter of Liverpool as it was possible to be at so close a range, and I could quite see why most of the Lambourn contingent, and plenty more besides, chose this as their launch-pad for the meeting. Some arrive on the Wednesday to acclimatize but for the majority, two nights of racing talk, revelries and precious little sleep, is enough. By the morning of the race, there are tell-tale signs of surrender on many faces, although this year at least one hardy group refused to be subdued. They had occupied stools at the bar for most of the preceding two days, one of them bellowing, at varying intervals, 'Three to one.' He was not pretending to be a rails bookie nor even claiming he was being outnumbered, but alluding to his choice of horse for the race, Ken Oliver's well-fancied Three to One. Minutes before I left for the course on Saturday, my own head feeling short of resistance to sudden noises, I saw them in the bar, breaking open a bottle of bubbly to set up the day. As I walked out through that old swing door, the roared strains of 'Three to One' followed me.

John Francome had shared a room with Phil Blacker on the Thursday night. Not being one for late nights and heavy drinking, he had eaten quietly in the mausoleum of a dining-room and retired to bed with a book. The champion, however, had spent a restless night and did not look his best at breakfast next day. Perking up only slightly to tease the elderly waitress belatedly clucking around us with a coffee pot, Francome explained: 'I hate being away from home, even for a night. It might sound odd, in this job, because we do so much travelling, but I always try to get back into my own house at night. In past years I have even driven home from Liverpool. Last night was depressing,' he went on. 'I am not a drinker, so I didn't fancy the bar, and I got myself really miserable sitting in that room after dinner. I'm checking out this morning because Miriam is coming up. She might not be too impressed with this place.'

Francome's mood was not helped by a chest infection which had been hanging around him for some weeks and seemed to be aggravated by each fall. He was paler than usual, and certainly quieter. It might also have been true that he was deflated by the prospect of losing his title to the young pretender, Peter Scudamore and, quite without malice, he told why he believed one incident had changed the course of the championship race. 'When I fell from Virgin Soldier at Newbury a few weeks ago,' he said, 'I was out for a couple of days and missed six winners. But at the same fence in that race, Sam Morshead fell from Mercy Rimell's Celtic Rambler – in fact it was him who brought me down. Sam's horse gave him a kick as he went down and punctured his lung, and he hasn't ridden since so almost all of the Rimell rides have gone to Peter. That's the difference between us.'

Francome confessed that he felt more like lying in some sunny spot for a week than chasing around the country in search of winners, but conversation soon flitted on to more agreeable subjects, like the title-chasing of his soccer favourites Spurs, the films of Jack Nicholson and the imminent concert tour of the gargantuan American singer Meat Loaf which John meant to attend.

He toyed with some poached eggs and studied the

Sporting Life with no discernible enthusiasm. Perhaps not surprising, as the best of Fred Winter's runners that afternoon, Fifty Dollars More, was to be ridden by Richard Linley because the owner, Sheikh Ali Abu Khamsin, had pronounced himself 'insulted' by Francome's preference for another of the stable's runners in a recent Cheltenham race.

Following the pattern of Francome's lean fortunes at this stage of the season, none of his own rides that day featured in the frame, and he was changed in time to watch Linley win comfortably on Fifty Dollars More in the last race. He hardly had time to feel sorry for himself, however, as within minutes of the race ending, news came through from Ludlow which was to give the racing writers plenty of scope for dramatic prose on the morning of the National.

The bad luck stories of Richard Head, Jenny Pitman and Oliver Sherwood pale when set against Phil Blacker's nightmare. Blacker had celebrated a little more than his room-mate Francome on Thursday evening, but he was still up, dressed and shaved in time to drive back down the M6 to Ludlow, where he had three booked rides for trainer John Edwards. Two were hurdlers and one, Durham Lad, would certainly start favourite for the penultimate race on the card, a handicap chase.

Jockeys, quite rightly, believe that if they cocoon themselves before a big race to avoid injury, they are just as likely to break their leg falling down the stairs. So they attempt to carry on much as normal and Blacker was simply carrying out the business which pays his wages and trying hard not to think of his ride on the National favourite the next day.

The two hurdlers were well backed but well beaten and Durham Lad ran disappointingly. He was fourth, with no chance of winning, when he blundered at the last fence, unseating Blacker, who landed on his head. It was the worst thing that could possibly have happened to him.

The course doctor had no option but to diagnose concussion and, under the Rules of Racing, Blacker was signed off for seven days. At the eleventh hour, he had lost his outstanding chance of winning the Grand National.

It caused an immediate rumble of interest at Aintree, which grew to a crescendo as poor Stan Mellor hustled unsmilingly from trainer to jockey and jockey to telephone, seeking an adequate, experienced replacement. Francome was offered the ride, with the blessing of Fred Winter, but declined to desert Rough and Tumble, placed twice in previous Nationals. Irish veteran Tommy Carberry was next to reject Mellor's approach, claiming to be too old, and so the mount went to Bob Davies, who was hastily recalled from his Gloucestershire home, having left Aintree before the drama unfolded.

For Stan Mellor, as for Lambourn, the agony of the National did not end there. Royal Mail fell at the sixth fence, the dreaded Becher's, and neither of the trainer's other two entries completed the course. Neither, for that matter, did all but eight of the thirty-nine, and the only Lambourn-trained horse to get round was a game twelve-year-old called Delmoss, trained by Fulke Walwyn and ridden by Bill Smith.

The race went to Grittar, ridden by an amateur, Dick Saunders, and as the oldest man to win the race and a close friend of the late John Thorne, he was an appropriate winner. The Lambourn roadshow took to the motorway once more, Aintree unconquered for another year, and the National Hunt season now with only its dying embers flickering.

11·Summer Holidays

H E looked pretty much the same as he had done eight months earlier, but if there were a few stress cracks in Nick Henderson's make-up as the season drew to its summer recess, no one could blame him. During that long and unforgettable winter he had suffered extremes of emotion in personal, not to mention business life. He had lost his father-in-law, John Thorne, in that most tragic of point-to-point accidents, but he had become a father himself when his wife Diana gave birth to a daughter in December. He had lost a jockey and then found him again and, on the course, he had lost rather too many races for peace of mind.

It was a hot and hazy May morning when I called. Nick was on the phone in his office, Sandra Bentick working efficiently through the files next to him. On the gravel outside in the sunny yard, a pram revealed the best news of the winter. All was well there, at least.

The phone snapped down. Nick looked up, smiled politely. He had forgotten our appointment. Not that it mattered, for although the phone continued to ring at regular intervals, the head lad occasionally poked his head around the door with anxious news of another equine patient and the greengrocer arrived with some apples, it was a comparatively lenient morning in the lifestyle of this particular trainer. He had only one runner that day, which his wife would ride in the evening meeting at Nottingham. 'She'll finish second, I reckon,' he said with a pessimism easily excused after the months he had endured but, in the event, unjustified. Lawn Meet won, and brought some cheer to the yellow house on

Hungerford Hill.

Nick looked as neat as ever in his roll-neck sweater. He was still, I noted, running his fingers through his hair and tapping his pen on the table. Nervous habits never die. He chatted generally, reserving his strong feelings for the state of Lambourn's roads. 'I reckon the trainers in Lambourn must pay around £100,000 a year in rates, and all we ask is decent surfaces for the horses to walk on. We get nothing,' he said with a trace of bitterness.

I asked him to look back through his season, and after an amused expletive and the protest that he could scarcely remember what happened yesterday, he did so. 'Up and down,' he said gloomily. 'You expect injuries in this game, but somehow it always seems to be the good animals who get hurt . . . probably because they are the only ones going fast enough. The biggest disappointment was a horse called Easy Fella going wrong. I really did rate him highly. But there were so many others.' He ran his pen slowly down his register of residents, putting a mark against all those who had broken down during the season. It was an alarming sight.

Did he ever feel like packing it all in and taking up a more relaxed profession? 'Never,' he laughed, 'because there is nothing else I could do. But you know, I always said I would never think of training flat horses, yet this season I have thought about it. It will get no further than this, but there are four very good reasons why it makes sense. The first is simply economy – there is more money to be made on the flat. The second is the weather. There would be less need to crawl out in the dark at half-past six on a December morning and have to fight through snowdrifts to get at the horses and feed them. Racing in the summer has its appeal. Then there is the inbuilt frustration of the jumping game. You have produced the horse in perfect shape, the jockey does absolutely every-thing right, goes ahead coming to the last, has the race won and then capsizes. Then you really do wonder why you are doing it. But the biggest reason of all for thinking of the flat is that injuries are so much rarer. I know flat trainers will retort that they suffer badly from viruses, but I still think there is nothing so galling as having a really good horse go lame in the yard just as he is ready to win a race.'

He made out a tempting case, but I sensed he was no more than half serious. Lambourn might be changing its emphasis, but there were some whose loyalty to the real racing sport would endure. I fancied Nicky to be one of them.

The season had three weeks left to run as we talked, but the weather had been so dry that only the firm ground specialists could run without risking more injuries. There were several in this category in the Henderson yard and he talked buoyantly of expecting a handful more winners yet. I admired his resilience.

'There is not much rest when jumping finishes,' he explained. 'As soon as the last meeting is over I have to think of Ascot sales, where we do most of our selling. After that I shall have ten days' holiday in France, before flying to Ireland for the sales there. The horses all come back in the yard at the start of July and, just as I'll probably have a runner at the final meeting at Market Rasen on 5 June, I am pretty sure to have one when racing restarts there on 31 July. It's funny to think that we have jumping all twelve months of the year now. There really isn't much time to laze around, as people imagine we have. But I'll play some golf with Fred. . . .'

The girl at the reception desk asked if I had an appointment, then called across the lobby to ask if anyone had sighted Mr Nugent recently. Not receiving an encouraging answer, she paged him over the tannoy system, and within a matter of minutes he burst through the door, managing to look rushed but unflurried, consulted his watch and apologized before vanishing again for ten more minutes. Life in Lambourn Garage, it seemed, was rather less sedate than in the workshop days of Frank Thatcher and old Sir Hugh.

'I can remember coming in here many times as a boy,' he smiled, on hurrying back to greet me. 'And this part of the reception area' – he waved precisely with his left hand – 'was the extent of the office premises. Everything was organized from here – the motor repairs, the horse transport and a certain amount of training business too, I dare say.'

Nowadays the administration centre is up a flight of stairs in a den of offices spread across a carpeted floor. Everything is spotlessly clean, an attribute still more noticeable in the office of John Nugent. He sits behind a wide desk on which nothing seems out of place. Files are filed, not scattered, and neat virgin pads are the only outward sign of activity. A plastic sign stands on the desk, its message adding to the impression of cleanliness and efficiency: 'Thank you for not smoking'.

Summer was drawing on, holidays were imminent, cars were being garaged for maintenance work before treks to the coast. But it was not, John assured me, noticeably busier than any other time of year. Just tolerably hectic. He summoned coffee from a well-dressed and discreet secretary, then talked of the Lambourn he had come to know and intended to make his home for the forseeable future.

'There have been changes in recent years, purely through the building of the M4 motorway. They were hectic times,' he recalled. 'They planned to run it right through the downs, destroying the racing gallops and probably destroying this village with it. We fought tooth and nail, and succeeded. We were the last motorway pressure group to win that kind of battle. Although the route was changed, to our advantage, it still had a major effect on this area, because it was suddenly so easy for people living here to commute to London each day. We became a dormitory for the capital, and since then the area has become more active, less dormant and set in its ways. I am not sure whether that is a good or bad thing, but I think Lambourn itself remains quite secluded.'

The flat-racing season was well under way and, despite his professed indifference to the sport, John was enthusing over the early successes of local trainers. 'Of course,' he said, 'I am delighted when things go well for them. They are my neighbours and friends, after all.'

That brought him to the subject which has griped for years in John's efficient mind, the age-old problem which makes Lambourn so eccentrically different from any other village in England. The horses on the roads. As I had again driven into the village that morning at 5 mph and on the wrong side of the road, to allow several strings of horses through, I was up to date with the size of the difficulty. But John contends that it should have been solved a generation ago.

'Since 1939, the county council have argued about providing horse tracks on the sides of the roads. There is ample room to do it, but for some reason best known to themselves they have never got round to it. I honestly don't know why there is not an accident here once a day. The council accept that fact but refuse to spend the money necessary to cure it, and there is nothing the parish council can do to force them. I fear it will need an accident to occur before anything is done, but if and when it is, it will revolutionize the place, save a good bit of agitation among motorists and apprehension among pedestrians.'

The opportunity to lay the tracks, he said, had often been passed by in favour of arguably less vital facilities. Personally, after a winter spent walking the streets and driving the roads of Lambourn, I wondered whether John might still be bemoaning the absence of horse-tracks in another twenty years, despite the ever-increasing amount of equine flesh in the place.

It would be unfair, however, to paint John Nugent as a

complaining militant. His life is so obviously a contented one, his influence so clearly for the good, and as he looked ahead to the summer he turned to such village issues as still matter in a society of hustling commuters and expanding business. 'We have a carnival each year, in August,' he reminded me. 'I resurrected it in 1973 when I was chairman of the council, and it still involves and attracts a great proportion of the village, which is good to see. But I recall in years gone by, we always had a Lambourn Festival Week, not just a one-day carnival which passes so rapidly. I would really like to see that return, and to see the village prepare for it as they used to.'

Like most of racing's heroes, Fred Winter is, physically, not much to look at. He seems small, even for a jockey, and in his glasses and woolly cardigan he could be one of the thousands of middle-aged husbands one passes without a second glance, doing the shopping on a Saturday morning. But the guv'nor of Uplands is far from ordinary; one of the legends of racing and the idols of my own boyhood, he has won virtually every major prize as rider and trainer and, so say all his acquaintances, not altered a jot through the glory.

I had left him until the end of the season, the end of the book, partly because I wanted him to look back and forward with that sharp brain of his and partly, I admit, through apprehension. Years of dealing with sports stars of all ages and qualities never quite removes the last traces of the intimidation that comes with hero-worship and I had always seen F. T. Winter as a figure much larger than life. I need not have worried. He answered the phone himself when I rang at 9.45 on 11 May. Uplands' first lot had just returned from their morning's work and Fred had been there with them, as he is every morning.

His telephone manner, one has to admit, would need some attention if he ever considered a career in the diplomatic service, but to meet the needs of a busy trainer who is at most times happy to allow his secretary or his assistant to deal with all enquiries, it is admirably noncommital. 'Lo', is the gruff ejaculation I was faced with, as is every caller lucky enough to get the man himself. But after some brisk preliminary introductions, he offered me an hour of his time at midday that very morning.

Uplands was looking a springtime picture. The garden which Fred and his wife Diana tend so lovingly during the summer months was already gushing with colour. The yard itself was spotlessly tidy and I was soon to be told how and why. Announced, loudly and joyously, by the family dogs, I met Fred and Lawrence Eliot at his front door. The boss was wearing a cravat and looking as dapper as ever as he smiled a greeting and ushered me through the kitchen, past the housekeeper, to the type of sitting-room in which one can feel instantly at home. There was the usual row of invitations on the mantelpiece – racing personalities seem to be in demand at all times of year – plus some prints and mementoes. The furnishings were soft and the design warm and friendly.

One particular print caught my eye as, sited above the fireplace, it was supposed to. It was an impression of a field of racehorses crossing a fence. All were properly equipped with saddle, reins and irons, but none had a rider. 'It's rather interesting, isn't it,' said Fred, pleased. 'Called "The Jockeys' Nightmare",' he chuckled.

He went off to fetch a cardigan, complaining of feeling cold. Since suffering a mild stroke two years earlier, he had taken things very much more easily, even agreeing to a mid-season golfing holiday with Josh Gifford on two occasions. 'I lead a quiet life these days,' he said.

A pretty fair-haired girl wearing a green and white rugby-style shirt wandered in. This was daughter Joanna, twin of Oliver Sherwood's new wife Denise. 'Ah,' said Fred, 'I've got something to show you.' He produced a gold ring which he said, had just been rescued from an unpleasant end in a wastepipe. It turned out to belong to

Diana, and Jo left to restore it to its rightful place. The hard professionalism which made him a great jockey and still makes him a great trainer, was temporarily invisible; this was more like the middle-aged husband in the Saturday shops.

Once conversation turned to business, however, I understood. Fred was plainly and deservedly proud of the way his yard was run, and likened it to an army platoon. 'I hated the army,' he pointed out, 'but I agree with their principle of delegation, and use it here. I am the company commander, Oliver is platoon commander. Brian Delaney, my head lad, is the sergeant major who sets the example to the troops and brings the inevitable few stragglers into line. Mick Cullen, the travelling head lad, is the sergeant.

'This place runs like clockwork, always to the minute – and when it fails, I want to know why. I am a great believer in routine, in everyone knowing their job and sticking to it. The lads know I will be with them every morning, and I shall continue to go out on the downs every day as long as I am able. But they are not so sure of my movements later in the day. I go round the boxes at evening stables twice a week – but I never tell them when I am going. It keeps them on their toes, you see.'

Fred Winter went into training as an afterthought. When he had finished his phenomenal riding career, he fancied a job inside racing and applied to be a starter, but no post was available. 'So I took a chance,' he recalls. 'And I went into it with a lot of doubts. I bought this yard from Doug Marks, who now trains up on the main road and remains my golfing partner. I've watched Lambourn grow, in racing terms, over recent years and I feel all the alarmist talk about racing is nonsense. A big fuss is made when any trainer goes out of business, but nobody comments when new trainers start up – and there have been plenty around here recently. The number of horses in training around Lambourn has trebled since I started, and there is never any shortage of willing owners. The money is around, no matter what people may say.'

I asked Fred if he liked Lambourn, as a home as opposed to a work base, and he made the distinction I had heard more than once in the preceding months. 'I love Upper Lambourn, where we live,' he said. 'It is divided from the main village by that little strip of, what, two hundred yards maybe, but it is separate all the same – and I like it that way. We are a little community on our own up here, because the road to Uplands is a dead end. We get the odd tourist in the summer coming to gaze at the place, but otherwise there is very little traffic. There has been a lot of building in Lambourn in the years since we came – and I still consider myself a newcomer so the changes won't seem so sharp to me. But, please God, the developers will not get into Upper Lambourn so long as I am around.'

The telephone trilled again. Fred was sitting in a favoured chair, his back to the front of the house and the yard, a view of the garden and beyond facing him. There was a telephone beside him and he seized it. 'Lo', he grunted, but the tones softened when the caller was identified as a lady owner, anxious to know why her horse had been withdrawn from the afternoon's meeting at Folkestone. All three of the Winter horses had been scratched after travelling down overnight, because Mick Cullen had telephoned to report the ground as dangerously hard. Fred was willing to take no more risks than necessary in this game with his treasured stable stock.

'Where was I? Oh yes, Lambourn. I really don't go into the village much, you know. No need. I prefer to stay at home. When I have been there, shopping, I don't suppose I have made regular visits to more than two shops. The newsagent's, of course, but everyone goes in there, and the chemist's on the corner opposite the betting shop. I think that chemist's is a lovely shop. They've got wine as well,' he said, breaking into another of those wide and unexpected grins.

We talked of the season just past, and Fred was satisfied. 'We have dropped slightly in winners from last year, but nothing to worry about considering how bad the weather has been. We are very near the £200,000 mark in prize money, which can't be bad really. I'm happy enough.'

Fred attends race-meetings less often than he used to, and probably less regularly than most of his training colleagues. He explained: 'I will go to any local meeting, within an hour and a half or so, and there are certain tracks I like to attend, like Fontwell. But I travelled so much as a jockey that the thought of sitting in a car for four or five hours doesn't appeal these days. It seems such a waste, anyway. I can chat to the owners when I get there, but I can do no more to make the horses win. Often I am much more use at home.

'When I do go racing, I wouldn't say I am emotional. I take a great pride in winning, of course, but it's not very professional for a trainer to scream and shout, is it? Anyway, both in terms of highs and lows, I take the view that nothing can happen now which hasn't already. Does that sound boastful? I do hope not,' he added anxiously.

Most of the other racing folk around Lambourn had cited Fred Winter among the best jockeys of their time, so now I put the question to the man himself. Who would he choose – and I did not have to add that he should exclude himself; I knew he would anyway. He thought silently for a minute or so and went to pour a drink – sherry with ice – before murmuring: 'I would say it is a toss-up between three. Bryan Marshall, Martin Molony and Johnny.'

For Winter to talk of Francome in the same category as his two great contemporaries was high praise indeed, and he expanded on it. 'Johnny has been a marvellous stable jockey. At times he is absolutely brilliant, probably the best of the lot. He has got everything. But there have been occasions when he has upset me, of course. He will go right round the outside, come in fifth or sixth and then jump off and say he's pleased. I have to bite my tongue then, because he is a sensitive bloke. But the silence on those odd days is worth it for the winners he has ridden which nobody else would have come close on. Everyone has bad days,' he went on. 'Steve Ovett has been beaten for no good reason. Jockeys are no different.' And Fred was off on another pet subject, that of athletes. 'I always watch the athletics on television and enjoy it. But I get annoyed when people make the analogy between horses and humans. If the world mile record is being broken so often, they say, why can't modern horses keep improving, too. The answer to that one is simple. Not so much time is spent on training the horses properly these days. Like everything else in modern life, there is a certain amount of rush, whereas the old-timers would train their horses to an absolute peak before running them.'

In that respect, Fred confessed with pride, he was old-fashioned. It had clearly not done him any harm, but as he ended his nineteenth season of training and his forty-third season in jump racing, how was his enthusiasm faring?

'At this moment, I am a dead duck. I am stale. I have had enough of this season, and I feel much the same every May. But I am rejuvenated each summer. All the horses are taken out during the summer, and during June this yard is like a morgue. It is quite pleasant for a while, but as soon as July begins, and the horses come back in, my interest revives. I like seeing how the old horses have done while they've been away, and normally, I will have eight or ten new horses to get to know. It awakens the competitiveness in me again, and I start thinking what I can do to make the new season better than the last.'

So nothing changes, it seems, and come the end of July, the little man with an unmatched touch for producing winners over jumps, would be back, heading for the top of the trainers' table again. In the meantime, he would have two weeks in Marbella, and, weather permitting, some long days with Diana and the dogs in his garden. Peace would reign at Uplands for the recess, with not so much as clopping hooves or Harry Foster to disturb it.

It was 84 degrees and rising, the windows of the Peugeot were down, the sun roof open and the stereo blasting out a Madness tape. In the driver's seat, the lean and pale young man loosened his tie once again. Behind him, a cheerful type with fashionably curled hair and a hooped sports shirt was repeating jokes heard at a dinner the previous night. The National Hunt season had twenty-four hours left to run and here, sharing a car in such obvious companionability, were the joint riding champions.

The car was a giveway. It was also an incongruous sight at Epsom, where the shirt-sleeved crowd was recovering from the Derby, looking forward to the Oaks and wondering why Peter Scudamore – for that was the name painted along the side of the white vehicle – had ventured to a flat-race meeting when, by his own admission, he had avoided racecourses since the gloomy Monday at the end of April when he broke his arm at Southwell.

There was a ready explanation. Scudamore had been twenty winners ahead of John Francome, and an unbackable favourite for the title, when fate overtook him for the second successive season. This time it had been his arm, the previous year a fractured skull. On both occasions, it seemed to have ended for another twelve months, his obsessive wish to be champion.

But not for nothing is jump racing known as the friendliest, as well as the most demanding of all sports. Francome's reaction had been spontaneous. He had phoned Michael Scudamore, Peter's father, and told him that he intended to work as he had never worked before in order to ride twenty more winners in the six weeks available to him. But if he managed to do so, if he drew level on 120 for the season, he would stand down from all future rides and share the title. Scudamore heard the news while lying in a Nottingham hospital, shortly after having two pins inserted in his wounded arm. He had been toying with the outrageous idea of riding again before the season ended, but now he abandoned the scheme and settled to wait. He never once went racing until it was over, but he followed every result as closely as if he himself had been sitting on Francome's horses.

Now the waiting was over, and it had been so long that the young pretender could not even bring himself to feel disappointed. Francome had caught him with two meetings to spare, but only by dint of a schedule in the season's penultimate week which might have left a rally driver exhausted

Up to then, he had continually insisted he had little chance. 'It gets harder and harder to find a winner,' he had said, with a fortnight left. 'I'm willing to go anywhere at the moment, but I can't see myself catching Peter.'

But, in two days, he drove more than a thousand miles, took in four meetings, rode five winners and closed to within one of the fretting leader. He started at Taunton, with two winners, on the Thursday night. From there, far in the south-west of the country, he drove north-east to Sedgefield, only just short of Geordieland, and rode one winner on Friday afternoon. Then, across the North Yorkshire dales to the north-west of England, and a first-ever visit to the cramped quaint track at Cartmel in the Lake District. One winner, Saturday afternoon, followed by a 250-mile dash to Southwell, east of Nottingham, and another success in the evening meeting.

Francome reached home shortly before midnight on the Saturday and confessed: 'I have never felt so exhausted. I hardly know what day it is any longer.' He pulled himself together enough to ride four favourites in the Bank Holiday Monday meeting at Fontwell Park in Sussex, where an enormous crowd was lured by the prospect of the title being decided. But Francome was beaten on all four, and trailed back to Lambourn wondering if he was still to be denied despite his debilitating efforts.

Finally, it was a modest novice chaser called Buck-master who came to Francome's rescue. Having already provided his winner at Sedgefield four days earlier, Buckmaster obliged in the 2.45 at Uttoxeter on 1 June. With great relief, and very little ceremony, Francome confirmed that he would not ride again and was happy to stick by his decision to split the championship with his friend.

So on the Wednesday night at the Sportsman's Club in London, Francome and Scudamore stood up separately at the National Hunt Awards, made their brief speeches and accepted their half-shares of the prize money. The following afternoon they both made the trip to Epsom to talk on television about the title and the point was put to Francome that he had let down the punters who had backed him for the title. 'I agree,' he said. 'But I did it for Peter, because I know how hard he had tried to be champion. It would have been unfair on him to lose everything in this way.'

They travelled back to Lambourn together, Scudamore on his way home to Stow-on-the-Wold but happy to divert and drop off his colleague. Francome was in prime form, his newly-styled hair swept up and back by the wind as we rushed along the M4, and his Wiltshire tones spilling out story after story. His passion for football was high, with the World Cup just around the corner. 'I played a couple of weeks ago,' he said, lapsing into the jokey style known so well by his riding colleagues, 'and I knew Ron Greenwood would want me in his squad, but it was a toss-up between going to Spain for him and entering for the French tennis championships.' I asked how he played. 'Oh, great. Every time I got the ball, the opposition started to run towards our goal. They knew I would pass it to one of them.'

Francome told how his wife had just acquired two baby ducks – 'not that we've got a pond for them to live in yet' –

and how she was still modelling clothes in London, but longing for home. 'We're going on holiday next week, a fortnight in Portugal. I can't wait . . . but I'll be back in time for Wimbledon.'

He sipped a can of cold drink and told some horrific stories of the dubious animals he had persuaded himself to ride in the final few days of his season. One was running at Stratford that night and Francome winced when I mentioned it. 'I have ridden some bad horses recently, but that one takes some beating. It was only after we had ploughed through the first fence that I realized I not only had no brakes, but no steering either. The bloody thing won, but if I was paid £1,000 I wouldn't get back on it.'

He was still chattering when he disembarked in Lambourn. Somehow, the place looks different in summertime. It was a hazy afternoon now and the village had an air of laziness about it. John Rodbourn was doing his rounds, stopping to chat with his many friends; the Catholic Club was holding a busy afternoon function; but in Upper Lambourn, at the controversial Cruck Cottage, all was still and sleepy.

A stable girl walked across the square, ice cream dripping down her chin. The laundrette was well filled with housewives, even the odd stable-lad, but the chip shop was shut, a notice announcing 'No Cheques' dominating its door. In Ladbroke's, the sun had clearly mixed with the alcohol in a few heads. Poor Sue Hawkins was battling vainly to calm an inebriated lad who was shouting hysterically about an unpaid bet. Outside, his shirt-sleeved mates passed round another bottle of cheap wine. The bank's alarm was whining like a New York police car, but nobody took the slightest notice. 'One day,' said Sue Hawkins in a quieter moment, 'it won't be a false alarm.'

Harry Foster was in the High Street, in his check cap and winter jacket, moaning about the difficulty of picking winners with as much fervour as his stables' jockey had earlier been complaining about the problems of riding them. Soon, he would go back to his house, sleep for an hour, cook his evening meal and then walk through the front door of The George on the stroke of nine o'clock. Nothing changes.

Round the corner, Wicks the saddler's was being tarted up with new paint and bold signs, and the lawn outside Barry Hills' stables was being cut by a mini-tractor. All modern conveniences for the village's biggest yard. Tomorrow, Hills was to run Last Feather and Slightly Dangerous in the Oaks, and Lambourn's money would be piled on them – or rather, on Steve Cauthen's chosen ride, Last Feather. But they finished second and third, the village's money was lost and there was nothing to celebrate. No point in ringing the church bells. No need for anger from the vicar, this time.

Index

Figures in bold denote main entries.